PRAISE FOR M
FOR CHANGE

"A step-by-step guide to reframe our relationship from generational to ecological wealth that centers the wellbeing of a society, culture, and planet. In our pursuit to become environmentally conscious in our individual purchases, we must also extend ourselves into community care that builds resilient systems for the future of societies. Kara's book is accessible, fun, and relatable for people to create a sustainable future."

—**Isaias Hernandez**, Founder, Queer Brown Vegan

"*Money for Change* presents an easy-to-follow, encouraging, and actionable blueprint for building your own sustainable financial house."

—**Stephanie Seferian**, author of *Sustainable Minimalism*

"Kara's book is a refreshing take on personal finance, focusing on sustainability and practical money strategies. It uniquely addresses how to balance our idealistic goals with the world we live in, offering clear steps to align our financial decisions with our values. This book is perfect for anyone looking to make their money work for a better, more sustainable future. Highly recommend giving it a read!"

—**Dasha Kennedy**, Founder, The Broke Black Girl

"The next time I'm in a financial-existential doom spiral, I'm going to curl myself around Kara's book. Kara does an incredible job of compassionately booping you on the nose with the truth, but then gives you tangible, creative action steps towards deflating the dark feelings. The biggest relief for me is that she isn't asking us to each build revolutions from the ground up; she lays out an accessible menu of options, from "How to find free sh*t in your community" to "Here's how to divest from Wall Street completely, for real." *Money for Change* is a map and a manual for how to do money and still sleep at night."

—**Berna Anat**, Founder, Hey Berna

MONEY FOR CHANGE

MONEY FOR CHANGE

HOW TO REDUCE WASTE, BUILD WEALTH, AND CREATE A BETTER FUTURE FOR ALL

KARA PEREZ

WILEY

Edition History
This book was previously published as *Green Money* © 2025.

Published by John Wiley & Sons, Inc., Hoboken, New Jersey.
Published simultaneously in Canada.

For general information on our other products and services or for technical support, please contact our Customer Care Department within the United States at (800) 762-2974, outside the United States at (317) 572-3993 or fax (317) 572-4002.

Wiley also publishes its books in a variety of electronic formats. Some content that appears in print may not be available in electronic formats. For more information about Wiley products, visit our web site at www.wiley.com.

Library of Congress Cataloging-in-Publication Data Is Available:

ISBN 9781394357178 (Paperback)
ISBN 9781394357192 (ePDF)
ISBN 9781394357185 (ePub)

Cover Design: Jon Boylan
Cover Image: © Eric Ferraz/Shutterstock
Author Photo: Courtesy of the Author

SKY10099584_030725

For everyone who believes in the beauty of the world, and every girl who was ever told she talks too much.

You all have a magic inside of you, and the world needs to hear what you have to say.

CONTENTS

INTRODUCTION

In June 2022, my partner and I declined to renew our lease in Austin, Texas, and booked tickets for a two-month-long trip to Mexico, Costa Rica, and Colombia. These were countries we had both long dreamed of visiting but had never had the chance. For the last three years my partner had been working full-time while going to school for his master's. I'd been building a business and trying to maintain it during a global pandemic. My partner had graduated just two weeks earlier, and I knew that if we didn't take this summer to do a big trip, we likely never would. He'd find a job and get three weeks annual vacation, max. Work would get prioritized, vacation time would get devoted to family trips, and I knew I'd regret not taking the opportunity when I had it.

We'd picked these three countries for two reasons: excellent hiking and a chance to practice our Spanish. Despite being half Dominican, my Spanish is intermediate at best, and my partner's is all learned from classroom settings. (He's got a great grasp of the grammar and a terrible accent.) Hiking, and just time in nature in general, is our favorite joint activity and what we plan most of our trips around. We're campers, kayakers, and wild swimmers. Something about being near trees, man, it just does it for us! The chance to hike in Oaxaca, Mexico, the rainforests of Costa Rica, and in the jungle of Colombia was basically a dream come true. Nature nerds, on a trip to celebrate and experience nature.

One afternoon in Costa Rica, we spent our afternoon at a beach along the Pacific side of the country. It was a short walk from our B&B, but we had to hop over fallen trees and brave a washed-out road to get there. When we made it to the beach, the view was stunning; a rock cliff dominated the left-hand side of the beach, and the ocean was a dark, deep blue that sparkled in the summer sun. There were two other groups of people there enjoying the space, and we strolled along the sand to find a spot to sit.

As we walked, I noticed that there was *a lot* of plastic waste on the beach. With every step I saw something new: a plastic fork missing a tong, one flipflop half buried in the sand, too many plastic water bottles to count. I mean the beach was almost as much plastic as it was sand.

I felt my anxiety start to rise. "Climate disaster," a tiny voice whispered in the back of my head. "You thought you could run from your eco-anxiety, but it's everywhere!" Even here, in one of the most eco-conscious countries in the world, which has done so much to protect and restore its native habitat, the impact of our climate crisis is evident. Our vacation here was to glorify nature, yet we kept seeing ways that nature was struggling. We found a spot to sit about halfway down the beach and my partner went for a swim. I took myself out for a walk along the beach, determined to collect as much trash as possible.

I didn't have a bag, so I found myself taking many trips out and back. One trip I devoted myself to just gathering plastic bottle tops, of which there were thousands. One time it was shoes—flipflops, Crocs, even two sneakers. Then I focused on the water bottles, making probably five trips to gather just them. I focused on getting trash nearest to the water, figuring that I was keeping it from being washed out that very afternoon. I cleaned a section of the beach over the course of an hour.

One of the groups that had been there when we arrived got up to leave sometime around my seventh trip. An older man, probably early 50s, spoke to me as he passed by.

"Thanks for picking up the trash," he said, giving me an approving head nod.

"No problem," I replied. "It drives me nuts seeing it."

But what really drove me nuts was this brief exchange. You see the trash too, dude! Why don't you pick some up? Why would you rather sit on a trash-filled beach than contribute to making it better? Do you think it's someone else's job? Do you not care?

This book is about how to use your money when you care while operating under a system that doesn't seem to. It's about how to align your dollars with your values. It's for people who know that we can use our money to create a more sustainable world, because the way we're currently doing things is not working. We're polluting the planet faster than we can clean it up, and we're warming the planet even faster. The Great Pacific Garbage Patch, the floating island of garbage that's just off the coast of California, is 1.6 million square kilometers, twice the size of Texas, or three times the size of France. The planet is on pace to hit 2.7° Celsius (4.9° Fahrenheit) of warming by 2100, less than 80 years from now. You will probably be alive at that point. Your kids will be alive. What won't be alive is many plants and animals. Agriculture crops are estimated to drop by anywhere between 5% and 12%. It'll be hard to grow corn in California if it only rains ten times a year in California.

I don't mean to bum you out, because this book is full of ways we can avoid that. It's a call to action through how we use our money because money is a tool for change. We're going to talk in depth about how we can all make small and big-picture changes in the world we currently have, because money is a tool for power. I'm not writing this book as a statement of doom and depression. I'm writing this book because I care, a lot, about our world and how we experience life on this wild and wonderful planet of ours. I want you to connect to your financial power and use it to help create the change we need.

I wrote this book because I want you to remember that we all live in nature every day, that we have made our whole lives here; nature is not some-thing that we drive to on the odd long weekend to go camping. Nature is your backyard, and the route you take to work. It's the coyote that runs across a four-lane highway and the bees that pollinate your vegetable garden. Nature is the tree that shades you as you wait for the bus, and it's the river in your neighborhood that dries up by the end of July every year. I wrote this book because we are killing where we live, and we're using a tool that we made up to do it. If we understand that tool better, and the systems it has created, we can save ourselves.

I want this book to help you think about money differently; it's not just numbers on a screen or bills in a wallet. It's power, it's agency, it's forward motion. I want you to be able to capture all that, hold it in your hand, and say, "Listen up, world. Here's how we're going to be doing things from now on."

When I took advanced placement government in high school, my teacher told my class that news producers had a saying: "Bleed in the lead." Meaning that as they assembled their evening broadcasts, the most shocking and usually negative story was given primary place. Look at any social media platform, and you'll see that habit repeated; rage-bait content, content designed to make us angry, unhappy, or sad, is always the best-performing content. I think this mindset flows easily into how we describe, highlight, and talk about money and our planet. We share stories of destruction, death, and despair; more people than ever are living paycheck to paycheck in the US, while at the same time the Amazon is being destroyed so we can plant more soybeans.

This limits and, in some cases, breaks our relationship to both our money and our world. Why care when everything is a mess? Why pick up the plastic trash on that Costa Rican beach when it will be replaced over the next three days?

Divide and conquer has been a reliable military strategy since we first started fighting each other. That's what's happening now, with us and our power. Money is a tool with great power, if you can harness it. Connection to others and the land around you is another tool. Reconnecting to it, and claiming it, can and will change the world.

I don't think a single person on the planet *wants* to live in a world with crop failure and plastic-filled beaches. I do think we live in a world where many of us are just far enough away from or confused by how everything works that we can't make the connections between our decisions and their impacts on the broader world. Most people want to protect our gorgeous and delicate world. Most people want to build financial security for themselves. Most people want to save the whales and the bees. They're just struggling with the gap between desire and behavior.

Throughout this book I've tried to break down how we can close the gap between the type of world most of us want and the one we currently have using money. Spoiler alert: usually it's information awareness, behavior, and personal circumstances. So throughout the book you will meet people who come from different backgrounds, races, genders, and financial circumstances and who are all working toward greener money for themselves and a greener world for us all.

I think there is a greater than ever before desire for change. More and more of us recognize that the way we are living is out of step with nature and our own desires. More of us want to work less and live more. More of us are exhausted by endless advertising. More of us are pissed at wealth inequality. More of us are pushing back against systems and cultural norms that only benefit a few at the top.

Covid especially pulled the wool from our eyes. We saw how fragile our consumer society is and how bullshit our workplaces often are. People learned that their jobs saw them as disposable, as only valuable when worshiping that modern god, profit. Gen Z largely says that they want to work to live, not live to work. The social and financial contract in the US has long been "work hard, and you will be rewarded with a house, a family, and financial stability." Less and less so is this the truth, with predatory student loan debt hanging around people's necks, high housing prices and high interest rates making home buying almost impossible, and a 15-minute ambulance ride clocking in at $4,000 for many Americans.

There is a collective questioning happening around the world: "Why play a game that you can't win? Why put the effort into a system where you are trapped in the struggle at the bottom while those at the top demand more and more for themselves?"

I answer that question in this book. It's a bit of a paradox; there are chapters where I will explain how to survive and thrive under this system, and chapters where I will invite you to help change this system. There are advice, information, and action steps in this book. Our world is beautiful and complex, and not all of us can make the same choices or have the same abilities. There's no one easy answer to all our challenges, and there's nothing I can say that everyone can implement. There is no universal financial or sustainability experience that we can all have, thanks to the differences in culture, money, ability, health, and lifestyle. That's okay! As zero-waste chef Anne-Marie Bonneau said, "We don't need a handful of people doing zero waste perfectly. We need millions of people doing it imperfectly." There's degrees of change, and this book explores those degrees, from personal financial choices, to community actions, to legislative change.

I hope that this book will guide you to imperfect green money. I hope it will educate you, inspire you, and most importantly, engage you. I hope you will be open to change and will bring your imagination to this book. That's the glorious thing about being open to new things; you have the opportunity to find freedom: freedom from fear, freedom from things that aren't working, freedom to meet new people and opportunities. Change often feels scary, but on the other side of that fear is a whole new world.

I want to see that world. And I want to see it with you. We're in this together, babes, even if we're all bringing something different to the table. In order to change our financial lives, our financial systems, and save the planet, we're going to need to work together. I don't want only one person to be cleaning the beach. I want all of us to clean the beach together and then sit back and say, "Damn. We did that. And look how cute this beach is now."

CHAPTER ONE

WHY CARE?

Everything is on fire but everyone I love is doing beautiful things and trying to make life worth living and I know I don't have to believe in everything, but I believe in that.

—Nikita Gill

I have been obsessed with money for the last decade of my life.

And for good reason: when I was 24, I was flat broke, desperately trying to find a full-time job, depressed, and struggling with my student loan payments. My full-time, posttax income that year was $16,100.

I felt that money was ruining my life. I was unhappy, earning an average of $1,000 a month living in Austin, Texas, and I was unable to do simple things such as go out for a drink without panicking that I would overdraft my bank account. I woke up in a breathless panic every night at 4 a.m., convinced I would be buried with my Sallie Mae paperwork. All my job applications were denied. Shame and embarrassment were constant companions. I felt like an absolute idiot for going to college and getting myself into student loan debt that I was struggling mightily to pay off. Financial stability, let alone financial safety, felt like a pipe-dream.

Money was a language that I didn't speak. I was drowning in self-doubt and in debt, and in a full-blown quarter-life crisis. Money dominated my daily thoughts, mostly playing in an endless loop of "Oh, my God, I am going to die broke, and I don't have enough to pay this bill, and I hate my life, and I'm a freaking idiot for doing this to myself." I needed something to change, so I did what any millennial would: I googled my problems. Typing "how to pay off student loan debt faster" into Google went from a digital distress call to a rally cry in about 24 hours. I discovered the world of personal finance bloggers who were sharing their stories of debt payoff, reaching early retirement, negotiating high-paying jobs, and I realized, "Oh, snap. Some people know how to do this money thing." And because ya girl is one stubborn and competitive lady, I decided that I would become financially fluent, come hell or high water.

Learning about money was a flashpoint in my life.

I dedicated myself to becoming debt free, cutting absolutely everything that wasn't necessary out of my life. Goodbye weekly $2 Tuesday friend hangs at Shangri-La, hello drinking tap water at home and watching The Sopranos on my roommates HBO account. Since no one wanted to hire me for a full time position, I sought out part time work, cobbling together five different part-time jobs. I worked some combination of these jobs seven days a week to increase my income. I hustled hard, working as a caterer, freelance social media manager, freelance non profit fundraiser, high school lacrosse coach, and freelance writer. I also took odd jobs, like nannying gigs and even once waited in line for someone for $150 cash.

I started to budget, obsessively. Whenever I got paid from one of my myriad jobs, I sat down at my computer and painstakingly allocated each penny of that paycheck to my basic needs and my student loans. I finally began to understand how to save and even invest my money. With this obsessive strategy, I paid off my last $18,000 in student loans in 10 months on my less than $20,000 a year salary.

Becoming financially fluent changed my entire world. Over a period of two years, my financial situation went from "drowning quickly" to "can now float." Where I had been stressed and overwhelmed by my student loans, I was now debt free. Where I had once had no cash savings, I now had $5,000 in my emergency fund. With each new financial milestone I hit, my anxiety decreased.

But why was money so hard in the first place? And why was I able to make such drastic changes, when so many other people in similar positions couldn't? These were, and are, questions that I wrestle with constantly. Why do some people have houses with 15 bathrooms and some people sleep on the streets in the richest country in the world? Why do some people get a rush from spending money, and others develop anxiety around spending? How come most of us spend most of our waking hours working to earn more money?

We're spending ourselves into an environmental hole and a mental health hole. When I was at my lowest income, I spent the most money. I spent a lot of my free time in Target, because Target is a fun, clean, and friendly place to be, and I was genuinely convinced that one more pretty notebook was the solution to my problems, instead of, you know, having more money to be able to actually afford my life. I didn't connect my brightly colored notebook with the idea that I was using shopping to find a sense of control in my very out-of-control life. In fact, I didn't think of my money outside of my own experience at all.

Which is a little strange, because money makes our entire world go round. Money is the key to modern life. Money, and specifically spending, has overtaken our whole lives and our whole planet in the past few decades. We need money to house ourselves, to feed ourselves, to clothe ourselves. We need money to take part in pop culture—you have to pay for HBO to watch the latest popular TV show, and you need money to buy tickets to see Taylor Swift live.

And the desire for profit, aka the money that businesses take home after all expenses have been paid, is what is fueling our global climate crisis.

Here are the financial facts: the average individual from a wealthy nation consumes 13× as much as the average individual from a poor nation. We have increased plastic production from 218 million metric tons in 2005 to 369 million in 2021 (UNCTAD 2022). Since the 1980s, we have built more homes with four bedrooms, while the percentage of two-bedroom homes being built has shrunk (US Census Bureau 2022).

A majority of Americans say that climate change is a major threat to the country's well-being, and 69% support the country becoming carbon neutral by 2050 (Tyson, Funk, and Kennedy 2023). In the US alone, 21 species went extinct in 2023, bringing the total to 671 species (US Fish and Wildlife Service 2023). As we make, buy, and ship more things, everything from water pollution to carbon emissions goes up. Carbon emissions set a new record high in 2022, hitting a global average atmospheric carbon dioxide of 417.06 parts per million (Lindsay 2024).

Today, we live in a world where 81 people have more money than 50% of the world. As of June 2023, the top 10% of US households held 69% of total household wealth. The bottom 50% of households held only 2.5% of total household wealth (Guzman and Kollar 2023, Hernandez Kent and Ricketts 2024, St. Louis Federal Reserve 2024). The official poverty rate in 2022 was 11.5%, with 37.9 million people in poverty (US Census Bureau 2024). There are websites that track billionaires' wealth growth. Type "spend Bill Gates' money" into a search engine, and a website will pop up that lets you spend $100 billion on everything from flipflops to farmland to NBA teams, just to demonstrate how much money this one dude really has.

At the root of the good, the bad, and the ugly of life today is money. We need it, but it's ruining our lives. We want to build wealth to protect ourselves, but hoarding money is causing huge problems. We want to look cute at our friend's summer wedding, but that dress was made by an underpaid woman in Bangladesh in unsafe working conditions. We want to take a vacation from Los Angeles to Dubai, but the carbon we emit will stay in the atmosphere for hundreds of years.

All of this seems overwhelming and, frankly, depressing. "It's all a mess," we tell each other. "What can one person even do?"

We Can Change

Things are the way they are because we make them that way. It's a sneaky truth that we often forget: nothing is permanent, and nothing has to stay the way it is forever. If we want to have fewer species go extinct each year, we can protect and preserve more land for them to live on. If we want to have fewer people living on the streets, we can redirect the money in the federal budget to build homes and provide health services.

To simplify it: anything that we make, we can make differently. I mean that in a "we can choose to use recycled material to make that T-shirt" and in a "we can spend $1 billion less on the military budget and put that toward building housing" kind of way. Everything about our lives is a series of choices.

I grew up low income, and continued to be low income until 29, when I finally broke into a middle-class earning. Throughout my first 24 years, before I had my quarter-life crisis, I didn't have very much money or any kind of financial education, but I had a lot of other things going for me. I was white, I was college educated, I didn't have kids, and I was able-bodied. That meant a lot of options were open to me, and if I started making some different choices, I had a very good chance of seeing different results. I didn't have to pay for childcare or take a job that allowed me to be home when my kids got off the bus, which meant I could work evenings at a catering company to increase my income. I never had anyone question my education, or make jokes about being a diversity hire only, which meant that I didn't deal with certain types of workplace discrimination.

The single most important thing for you to know is that the world is the way it is because of the choices we make every day. Nothing is set in stone; nothing is preordained. If you decided not to go to work for the next three days, that would change your life. (You'd probably be fired.)

If we decided to set federal price limits on insulin, that would change the budgets of millions of Americans. (They'd probably save money.)

These changes might be short-lived or long-lasting. But they are the direct results of new and different choices made at both personal and systemic levels.

Take that, and zoom out, and you basically have our entire world. Everything, from how we earn money to where we spend it to the clothes we wear to the movies we watch, it's all the result of choices being made, actions being taken, and those effects compounding as we do the same thing over and over again.

When I was broke and financially uninformed, I spent the most money. It's expensive to be broke! I paid extra in things such as credit card interest because I couldn't pay off my bill in full each month. Plus, I was mainlining endless television shows and social media posts about how other people were spending lavishly and being told that that's what success looks like. It was nonstop comparison of my broke and sad life to people who were jetting off to Italy for the summer. *Why wasn't I like them? What was wrong with me that I couldn't figure this money stuff out?*

For most people in the US, money is our number-one source of stress. A 2023 study from Deloitte found that among Gen Z and millennials, finances and the well-being of their family was the number-one stressor (Deloitte Global 2023). Money is the number-two reason for divorce. We need money to house ourselves, feed ourselves, and clothe ourselves. Money runs our world, affects our mental health, and shapes the industries around us.

So it stands to reason that if we can change our money, we can change not only our personal lives *but the very world that we live in.*

WE'VE ALREADY DONE THIS, ACTUALLY

In 1791, English abolitionists stopped buying sugar. Sugar at the time largely came from the West Indies, today known as the Caribbean, predominantly the modern-day countries of Jamaica and Barbados. The people who grew and harvested the sugar that Brits sprinkled into their tea and baked into their scones were largely enslaved Africans and Afro-Carribeans.

Caribbean sugar plantations were infamous for their inhumane working conditions, and enslaved people at sugar plantations had a 50% higher death rate than those at coffee plantations.

In 1791, abolitionist William Fox published a pamphlet urging a boycott of slavery-produced sugar, and this piece of writing went on to become the most popular pamphlet *of the century*. Fox wrote, "If we purchase the commodity, we participate in the crime. The slave dealer, the slave holder, and the slave driver, are virtually agents of the consumer, and may be considered as employed and hired by him to procure the commodity ... In every pound of sugar used we may be considered as consuming two ounces of human flesh."

Strong words that carried a strong impact. That same year, an English merchant named James Wright published a newspaper ad to explain why he would no longer sell sugar until he could procure it through channels "more unconnected with Slavery, and less polluted with Human Blood." Women, who could not yet vote to abolish slavery, participated through their economic power. They promoted the sugar boycott to their friends and family, refusing to spend household money on any slave-produced sugar. The British boycott, at its height, had more than 400,000 participants.

The cause was disrupted by the French Revolution, but in the 1820s, a British Quaker woman and abolitionist named Elizabeth Heyrick quietly decided she was absolutely done with sugar grown and harvested by enslaved people in the Caribbean.

Elizabeth returned to using the economic approach in her desire to see slavery abolished. If sugar plantations used slave labor, she would stop buying sugar and encourage others to do so as well. In 1824 she published a pamphlet titled "Immediate, not Gradual Abolition or An Inquiry Into the Shortest, Safest, and Most Effectual Means of Getting Rid of West Indian Slavery." It sold thousands of copies in Britain and the US. Her argument was simple: boycott goods produced by slavery and companies that used slave labor would be forced to stop if they wanted to survive.

"Let the produce of slave labor henceforth and forever be regarded as 'the accursed thing' and refused admission to our houses," she wrote. "Abstinence from one single article of luxury would annihilate the West Indian slavery!!"

Together with another woman, Susannah Watts, Elizabeth started a grassroots campaign and went door to door in her town of Leicester to promote a boycott of West Indian sugar. By the following June almost a quarter of the town's population had given up sugar. This economic action raised the issue of slavery with people in England, who lived more than 4,000 miles away from the sugar plantations. The Haitian Revolution succeeded in freeing Haiti from French rule and ending slavery in 1804, setting off a chain reaction against slavery within the Caribbean. In 1833, the British Parliament passed the Slavery Abolition Act, freeing more than 800,000 enslaved Africans in the Caribbean, South Africa, and Canada.

The Haitians had fought for their freedom with blood and steel. William Fox and Elizabeth Heyrick both used money to send a message to sugar companies and their government: *we will not stand for your behaviors. Let go, or be dragged into the future.*

If you've ever looked around and said, "Why is that thing the way it is? It doesn't really make sense, and it could probably be better if we did it this way instead," you're in the right place.

Because, simply put: we have the power to change everything and make life awesome. And we should take it.

WHERE TO START WHEN EVERYTHING FEELS BROKEN

When I open TikTok there's a 50% chance the first video I will see will be someone talking about a very serious, very painful problem that our world currently faces.

Amani, from AmaniTalks, is likely to tell me that men treat women poorly in romantic relationships and share ways that women should stop engaging with this bad behavior.

Carissa, from Carissa and Climate, can pop up with a video about how the warming of the oceans is killing sea life at a deeply concerning rate.

Not Just Bikes may have a video about a pedestrian death caused by our car-centric culture and poor urban design that makes walking unsafe.

These are important but not fun videos. I want to engage, but I also want to see a cat try and climb a Christmas tree, you know? I want to see a baby seal cuddle up under its mother's flipper and then flip-flop its way to the ocean for a swim.

I want to be part of the solution. But I want to have a moment of peace. I want to engage with the problems we're all grappling with, but I want to be able to enjoy my one wild and precious life (to quote Mary Oliver). Where is the balance? How can we watch cute baby seals and defeat misogyny? How can we save the polar bears and shake our booties at the club?

Let's start by looking at what's in front of us. Financial and climate challenges do not look the same across the world. People tend to think that climate change is one big bad thing that will happen all at once. We'll all go out, as a species, as the dinosaurs did. One fell swoop of disaster, and then silence.

But climate change already is, and will continue to be, a series of small disasters that impact certain people at certain times. We will not experience the same impacts, in the same way, at the same time. Cape Town, South Africa, will run out of water while San Diego residents ring in the Fourth of July in 110° heat. Northern England will experience flooding from heavy winter rains that wipe out their roads, while Pakistan struggles with drought killing their farming crops. The Dominican Republic will see stronger and more frequent hurricanes while Massachusetts winters grow shorter and warmer.

How the climate crisis affects you will depend on who you are and where you are. Wealthy white people in Silicon Valley will have more resources to utilize than garment workers in Bangladesh. We are all in this together, but we are not all equally vulnerable.

Where are you in the world? What are the challenges in your community? That's where you start. Yes, we have global problems, but where we start is with local solutions. And if you are reading this and live in a wealthy, Western country, your actions matter *a lot*, to both your local community and halfway around the world. In 2022, global greenhouse gas emissions from the top 10 countries with the highest emissions accounted for almost two thirds of the global total—those countries include China, the United States, India, the EU27, Russia, and Brazil. The countries producing the most emissions are the countries least likely to deal with climate-related disasters. People living in wealthy Western countries have an extraordinary opportunity to change the course of climate disaster by changing what they do with their money.

My partner and I moved from Austin, Texas, to Charlotte, North Carolina, in February 2023. We were excited to leave behind the Texas summers (try four straight months of 110-degree days, and let me know how you like it) and looking forward to having access to the Smoky Mountains since we're dedicated hikers. What we were not looking forward to was having to make friends in a city where we only knew one person.

Once we returned the U-Haul and hung our art on the walls of our new apartment, I got down to the business of making friends. In my 20s in Austin, I had made friends by being in proximity to people. My roommates were my friends, my catering coworkers were my friends, my small business colleagues were my friends. It had worked, but it didn't have purpose, and more than once I had found myself out of alignment with someone I called a friend. In Charlotte, I wanted to be values aligned with our new community from the start.

So once again, I turned to Google. I searched "sustainability non profits in Charlotte" and found several that piqued my interest. The one that spoke most to me was one about planting trees. As a nature nerd, I figured this was something that would be good for the planet (trees absorb carbon, which is hugely helpful in slowing global warming), and it was time spent outside and away from Instagram (my technology addiction).

New volunteers for this organization had to go through a classroom training, which detailed the history of the tree canopy in Charlotte, as well as the type of trees that were most beneficial to plant for the local ecology. And in the classroom training I found out a startling fact: almost all of the trees in Charlotte today were planted by humans in the 1920s and 1930s.

I had assumed that there was a forest here, and then humans came, chopped down some trees to build homes and businesses, and left some trees for shade and scenery. I assumed the trees had had dibs on this area. I was wrong! Turns out this area had largely been treeless when it was colonized by Europeans in the mid-1700s. White settlers built houses and roads in large open areas with trees brought in from miles away, and no one cared that much about tree coverage. That is, until the late 1800s, when people started talking about how bad the windstorms had become and how hot the city was in the summer.

Without a strong tree presence, the entire city was at the mercy of strong winds and hot sun. There were few tree branches to provide shade for people walking along sidewalks and no tree barrier to slow wind storms. So city developers decided to do something: they would transform Charlotte into a city filled with trees. They partnered with landscape architects to design new tree-lined roads and lush canopy over the streets, sidewalks, and lawns. They transported trees from nearby forests and planted them in Charlotte.

And the city changed. In 2022, 47.3% of Charlotte land was covered by tree canopy (that means tree trunks and the space that tree branches cover) (Trees Charlotte 2022). There are major parks with trees scattered throughout the city. From the decision and effort of a group of people 100 years ago, a new city has been brought to life and maintained. People have enjoyed Charlotte's trees for decades. And now people like me help plant new trees and care for the old ones so we can sustain a green city.

This is important work, not just because trees are cool. North Carolina, just like the rest of the world, is being affected by climate change. The state is experiencing hotter and drier summers. More people are moving to Charlotte, putting pressure on the water systems. By planting trees around Charlotte, I am taking climate action in my literal backyard. I am helping to cool the city down, since trees both provide shade from the sun and capture carbon before it gets stuck in the atmosphere. I'm helping keep the city walkable, since a cooler city means people can walk outside in the hotter months instead of being stuck in an air-conditioned car.

While climate change is a global issue, our starting efforts should be local. So what is your "tree planting"? What issue do you want to get involved in? What is near to your heart? What do you have the time for?

MONEY IS A TOOL FOR CHANGE

Okay, but what if you have three kids at home, or work 70 hours a week, or have a mobility limitation, and you don't have time to frolic around planting trees? What if your life is not a mirror image of mine? What can you do? What's in your power?

For the remainder of this book, we'll be taking a financial focus to the idea of sustainable living and what to do in the face of climate change. If you're anything like 24-year-old me, you know money is important, but you can't seem to grab ahold of it in your own life.

That's because money is a tool, and right now, most of us don't know that. For people without money, money seems to be the enemy itself, as if money itself were out to get you, as if money were plotting against you, finding ways to sneakily leave your bank account so that you get charged a $35 overdraft fee when you're simply trying to pay for groceries.

But money is literally a thing that we made up.

Think about how freeing and weird that is for a second. Money is made up. We, as people, decided we liked shiny, pretty gold, and we made it valuable. Then we did the same with jewels and silk, and all sorts of other things, and we invented whole systems of how much this amount of metal would be worth to us.

And then we built nations around it. Isn't that wild? We did that.

But now, roughly 5,000 years after the first version of money was exchanged (the shekel, in Mesopotamia), money runs our world.

In the US, we wake up, and we go to work every day. Why? To earn money.

And then we use that money to pay for our lives, like our car insurance and our Trader Joe's snacks, and the video game we just bought for our 12-year-old. We book flights to see family on the other side of the country, and we send money orders to family back in the old country. We pay the phone bill so we can text our moms, and we buy a six-week pottery class to reignite our creative spark.

Money is the common thread through all of our lives, our choices, our goals, our fears, our problems. Our relationship to money, and the amount of it we have, enables us to live our lives. Or, if you don't have money, it restricts our ability to do things.

For example, we literally let people simply live outside because they don't have enough money to pay for housing. That's the core root of what people call the homelessness epidemic. Housing in the US is what we call a "hot commodity"—meaning it's something for sale that a lot of people want.

That's what a commodity is—a primary material that can be bought and sold. Copper is a commodity—we use it to make pipes and put those pipes in houses. A commodity is something essential that we use to make other things. Referring to housing as one means it's popular and it's essential to the making of a life.

But if you don't have enough money, housing ain't for you! Seems like a problem, right? Not only does it lead to hundreds of thousands of people without homes, but homelessness also exacerbates problems such as litter, unsanitary drinking water, and overcrowding of public places.

Here's the sneaky little secret about using money as a tool: we can all use money to fix problems as much as we can use money to create problems.

That's what Vienna, Austria, has done with its housing. Vienna topped *The Economist*'s list of Most Livable Cities in 2024, 2023, 2022, 2020, 2019, and 2018. The streak is largely built on its infrastructure, such as housing, walkability, and cost of living.

Vienna has a robust housing program that helps ensure that no matter what your income level, job title, or health situation are, you can have housing in the city.

Vienna is both a city and a province in Austria. Vienna has the right to change tax law for its residents, which it did in order to provide affordable and safe housing.

Starting in 1918, after the ending of World War I, Vienna enacted a series of high taxes on everything from dog ownership to car ownership in order to fund the building of new affordable housing. Housing was desperately needed: after the war, people were sharing rooms in shifts, often in older buildings without indoor plumbing, windows, or safe fire exits.

The money raised by the city, in tandem with people leaving the city and selling property in a post-war economy, meant that Vienna as a city became the sole owner of huge parcels of land across the entire city. And ever since then, Vienna has been building mixed-use housing and affordable housing.

The Wohnpark Neue Donau housing project is built along the Danube River and consists of 850 apartments spread across one-, two-, and three-bedroom units. Rents are regulated by the city government so that none of the residents pay any more than 20% to 25% of their household income for housing.

This system means two things: the people living in the project can come from various financial backgrounds. You are as likely to find someone making $110,000 a year as you are $300,000 in this building. It also means that if you make $25,000 a year, you'll never pay more than $6,250 in rent annually. If you make $100,000 a year, you'll never pay more than $25,000 in rent annually. Having these caps means that people can safely save according to their income, thus building personal financial security. They can know that they will have housing they can afford year after year, because their rent will never outpace their income.

Building on that feature is that Vienna's income restrictions for subsidized units only apply when families first move into a unit. Residents are never required to move out, even if household income levels increase in the coming years. This arrangement results in a substantial number of moderate-income residents living in subsidized housing, and this mixing together of residents with different income levels helps with social integration.

In the US, we largely have financially segregated neighborhoods and even financially segregated towns and cities. If you can't afford to live somewhere, you probably don't work, play, or generally spend time there. Take the city of Wellesley, Massachusetts. In 2022, the median household income was $250,000. In April 2022, the median single-family home price was $1,870,000 (Wellesley Housing Development Corporation 2022).

In Wellesley, 97.4% of households had a computer in the house, and people living in poverty were reported at 4.1% of the population (US Census Bureau 2022). There are precious few people making $40,000 a year or under in Wellesley, because they can't afford to live there.

In Vienna, since the city has a large amount of affordable housing and a robust plan to keep creating affordable housing, middle-income or high-income residents typically do not crowd out lower-income residents. The city continues to add new subsidized units annually, at a pace of about 5,000 per year. This means that housing and neighborhoods do not become financially segregated into homes for the haves and have-nots. The stigma of being "low income"—or God forbid, "poor"—is avoided, and people are constantly surrounded by people outside their immediate income bracket, while people at various income levels are housed year-round.

Vienna made a choice to provide housing for its people. It's a choice that can be made anywhere, at any time.

SO WHY CARE? CHANGE IS THE ONLY CONSTANT

In July 1845, Henry David Thoreau took to the woods, famously writing, "I went to the woods because I wished to live deliberately, to front only the essential facts of life, and see if I could not learn what it had to teach, and not, when I came to die, discover that I had not lived." (I must note here that his mother would continue to do his cooking and laundry for him for the two years he was writing at Walden Pond.)

In April 2020, about a month and a half after Covid-19 forever changed our lives, retail sales dropped 16.4% (Cox 2020). Our norm had been disrupted; in-store shopping and eating in restaurants had become a scary and dangerous activity that could literally kill us.

Always, always have there been people compelled to change the way they live. Always have there been incidents and shocks that pushed people toward large-scale change. Today we are living more of the same. The shock is the greatest one humans have yet faced; we are truly in the fight for our own survival. But humans, as a group and as individuals, have done almost nothing but change continuously for the entirety of our history.

Around the world humans have a rich history of saying, "Fuck this" and pushing for better for themselves and the future generations.

As I write this in Charlotte, I am wearing a pair of jeans that were made in Vietnam. I will bike to my gym later today on a bike made in California. I have a snack of Trader Joe's turkey Chomps and mandarin oranges, both grown or produced hundreds of miles away from where I live. Our world is interconnected in millions of ways. We are all connected, and the decisions we make echo through our immediate life and the lives of people across the global supply chain.

And that means that our money has power. Every decision we make, from where we bank to what we invest in to how we shop, has the chance to make a true impact on the shape of our world. When enough people in England and the Caribbean got pissed off about slave-produced sugar, the British Empire bent to their will. When enough people in Charlotte got sick of not having trees around them, they planted millions in their own backyards.

WHAT ELSE AM I DOING?

This is the question that I ask myself when I think about working on large-scale problems. What else am I doing, really? I mean in life. I'm sending emails, I'm creating content on social media, I'm reading library books, I'm planting trees, and I'm watching reruns of my comfort shows, mostly. So yes, I do have the time to set up a home compost situation.

The time will pass anyway. The world will see 2050 and 2100 whether or not we do anything today. Time marches onward.

But what kind of a world we will have in 2050 and 2100 very much depends on the actions we take today. The science is clear: 2100 will be a *bad time* if we don't change course. There will be a severe lack of water across the planet, sea levels will have risen and wiped out coastal cities, and the global temperature will be so high, winters will no longer have snowfall.

It's a world where survival will be hard and resources scarce. But this world is not a foregone conclusion. We do not have to accept that future as the only option for ourselves and our children. We can change our present-day world and thus change the future for every single person on this wild and beautiful planet of ours.

And it all starts with our money.

CHAPTER TWO

QUESTION SYSTEMS, DON'T BLAME PEOPLE

And one day we must ask the question, "Why are there 40 million poor people in America?" And when you begin to ask that question, you are raising questions about the economic system, about a broader distribution of wealth. When you ask that question, you begin to question the capitalistic economy. And I'm simply saying that more and more, we've got to begin to ask questions about the whole society...

—MLK, Atlanta, Georgia, August 16, 1967

H uman brains are a funny thing. We have built wondrous things such as the Roman aqueducts, and we have sent people to the Moon, but we tend to struggle with thinking outside our own lived experiences. Most of us believe that the way things are now is the way things have *always* been. People are often shocked when I say capitalism has only been around for about 500 years. What we know is what we are comfortable with. In a somewhat darkly ironic twist, humans generally don't react well to new ideas and new ways of doing things, despite that often being the solution to our problems.

Our world today is made up of systems and rules. There are economic systems, social systems, and political systems, and they all work together to create a series of rules that people live by. You can't walk around naked, because we have laws against public nudity. You can't get a mortgage for a house without a credit score, because we have an economic system that requires credit history to be granted a loan. You can't yell "Fire!" in a crowded theater, because we have a social contract that says you don't unnecessarily scare the crap out of people in shared public places. All of these systems work together to shape the choices we make. If you live in a monarchy where the king has supreme power and the king says, "Hey, everyone has to serve in my army," you have three options: you can flee your home country, you can serve in the army, or you can go to jail. These are your options under that system.

Three quarters of Americans want to see government action on climate change, yet systemic change has been almost nonexistent in our country (Tyson, Funk, and Kennedy 2023). We haven't transitioned away from fossil fuels, we haven't embraced green energy, we haven't invested in climate-resilient lifestyle practices. We have been trained to look away from the oil companies leaking oil into the Gulf of Mexico and to hyperfocus on the actions of individuals. Rather, we're told, "It's your use of 14 plastic straws a year that is the real problem, not the fact that in 2019, Exxon Mobile created 730 million tons of carbon dioxide emissions alone, approximately the same amount as the entire country of Canada" (ClientEarth n.d.). We're being gaslighted while the global temperature continues to tick upward.

Often it feels as if we're staring the problems right in the face and then doubling down on the things that are creating disastrous climate change.

The US was the world's top producer of crude oil in 2018–2022, a time when we had already begun to live with climate disaster (US Energy Information Administration 2023).

There's a disconnect in our systems, a gap between what most people want and the systems we actually live within. Most of us know something is off with the way we are currently living and working, but we often struggle to change it. Who can protest fossil fuel companies when rent is due? Who can redesign capitalism to be more fair when your three-year-old has to go to the doctor this week, and the car is making a weird noise?

Change is essential, but *what* should we change? And what should we be trying to become? In order to understand what we need to change today and where we need to go in the future, we have to look at how we got to the present.

HOW DID WE EVEN GET HERE?

Most American thinking around ownership and money can be traced back to class struggles and the economic shift from feudalism to enclosure in England between 1067 and 1500. You're probably somewhat familiar with feudalism; images of King Arthur might pop into your head, stories about knights, kings, and serfs all living among each other. But what you might not know is how that led to a period called "enclosure," and how enclosure would eventually birth capitalism.

After William the Conqueror sailed over from Normandy, France, and defeated King Harold in 1066, William instituted feudalism as his legal, social, and economic system. Under feudalism, William granted knights and barons land in return for their fighting alongside him during his battle for the throne. These people were the king's vassals—under feudalism, all land technically belonged to the king, but vassals held land in their names and paid the king for the pleasure of doing so. Serfs worked the land under the vassals, and in return they were entitled to legal protection from the vassals and the right to work to feed and house themselves on the vassals' land.

Serfs were bound to the land they lived on. They lived and worked on lands owned by their local lord, but they were required to pay a portion of their overall annual labor to their lord. So if, for example, a serf grew and harvested 100 pounds of wheat on land owned by the lord, the lord would collect a tax of 15 pounds of wheat from the serf, since the wheat had been grown on their land.

Serfdom was not a good deal for the serfs. They didn't own the land they worked, and neither could they leave the land without permission from their lord. Their labor fed and housed the lord, and they had to repeat the same labor to house and feed themselves. The system was kept in place via both economic and violent means; landholders would kidnap freemen to become serfs if they needed them, and serfs couldn't become freemen without buying their way out.

This system chugged along for about 200 years, with regular moments of protests from serfs that would be put down violently. Then the Black Plague hit the continent, and between 1346 and 1353, killed roughly 50 million people in Europe. Some estimate that 50% of Europe's entire population died. What happens to a society when half of the population dies? Put simply: things come to a crashing halt.

There were fewer people to farm the fields, fewer people to make the clothing, fewer people to hunt. People didn't want to go near one another for fear of catching the plague, and entire villages were deserted. Lords couldn't protect their serfs from the plague, cracking the belief system that the rich and royal were blessed by God and thus deserving of serfs' labor. With fewer people to do anything, the feudal system collapsed. Serfs stopped paying their lords and began to fight for their rights to, for example, own the land they worked daily.

And a logical thing happened; with a severe lack of workers, a new distrust of the entire social contract between serfs and lords, and a new abundance of land without clear ownership, serfs no longer wanted to be serfs. A series of revolutions happened throughout England in the 1300s, and by the 1380s serfdom had collapsed in England. A new social system emerged, where former serfs became landowners themselves or collectively worked together to grow food from the same piece of land for multiple people. Wages rose, forests that had been decimated under serfdom regrew, and women earned more money and were granted the right to own property.

From a horrendously unfair system grew a much more fair, equitable, and most importantly, ecologically sound system. The law of the divine right of kings and lords had once ruled the entire continent of Europe, and now the common man had power in their own name. Private ownership of land fell, and forests and fields became openly held, meaning everyone had access to use them. Anyone was free to hunt, fish, and farm on land that had once been controlled by one lord. Fewer people had to pay taxes in the form of food or labor to someone higher up than them in the hierarchy. Historians refer to this roughly 150-year period as a "golden age" of Europe's proletariat (Hickel 2020).

It was pushback to this period of proletariat power that gave birth to the form of capitalism that we know now. The former lords and kings didn't take kindly to losing their power and free cash flow from the lower classes. Around 1500, as the population had recovered from the Plague, pushback to peasant rebellions began to take very violent turns. Revolutionaries were slaughtered, peasants were hung, and nobles began to take back private ownership of the land.

This was the birth of capitalism as we recognize it today. We call this period of time "enclosure" because the nobility actually enclosed the land. They forced people off the land they lived on, burned down their houses, and literally put up fences, walls, and armed guards to keep the land private. The farming economy that had prevailed after serfdom was crushed; peasants lost the ability to trade with each other and were forced to sell their time and labor working on the now privately held land for wages in order to pay for their food and housing. Does that last part sound familiar?

From enclosure came the idea that people should work in order to be able to purchase their living essentials. While under serfdom, serfs had been forced to work land they didn't own to survive, they largely didn't have to pay for things such as food or housing. Enclosure created the earliest version of capitalism, where non-owners were forced to work in order to afford things that kept them alive.

This economic system of private ownership was further entrenched by the legal system. In 1530, the English Parliament passed the Vagabonds Act, where homeless people could be whipped simply for being homeless. In 1597 another Vagabond Act was passed, which created penal camps for homeless people. If you were homeless, you could now be arrested and sent off to a work camp, where your labor benefited the state. The acts criminalized not working and not having a home, forcing people into the system of selling their time for money.

Coming back to the present, today we live under systems that are the descendants of that same structure: basic necessities to staying alive such as housing, food, and health care are all things that must be paid for via trading your time for money. The main idea is still the same; I own this thing that you can pay me for access to. Or I own this thing and will pay you as little as possible to turn it into something else that I can then sell for much more money, and I will keep the difference because *I originally owned the thing*. We call this system "capitalism."

Capitalism is an economic and political system in which a country's trade and industry are controlled by private owners with an emphasis on making as much profit as possible. That's why Amazon pays workers $15 an hour and posted $30.4 billion in profit in 2023. Amazon's goal is to get as much work out of each employee at as low a paid rate as possible, and then to sell the items their employees create at as high a price as possible, and to keep the difference for the shareholders. This system is why Jeff

Bezos, the founder and biggest shareholder of Amazon stock, has around $200 billion to his name.

Ownership is the key to capitalism, much like it was the key to enclosure. You can only win if you own something: a piece of land, a valuable skill set, or money itself. People who have skills deemed valuable are paid more money for their time, and people who have skills deemed low value are paid less. The value of a skill is generally determined by education required to gain the skill, gender of the person with the skill, and how long they've been performing it. (Brain surgeons make far more than sanitation workers, though no one wants to live in a world without weekly trash pickup.)

We also use the law to uphold capitalism and provide workers, just like England did with the Vagabond Acts. Our society doesn't provide basic necessities, such as housing and food, to people just because they are people. You have to work, and crucially, you have to *earn enough to pay market rates* set by the owner class, in order to access these things. In the US, 48 states have laws restricting the movement of unhoused people, banning them from parks, benches, and even sitting down in public places. In Texas, a homeless person can be fined $500 for camping in public places (National Homelessness Law Center 2021). We have criminalized simply existing because the goal of capitalism is that every person spends as much time as possible working to create profit for the owner class.

Knowing our history is important. It does us all a major disservice when we buy into the lie that how we currently live is how all humans have always lived. It robs us of thinking of how we might change things. History sets the stage for what might come next; by looking backward we can see the problems and advantages of how we got here. Zooming out and looking at our systems top down, it seems that the obvious question we have to ask ourselves is, "Why do we punish individuals instead of changing systems?"

Fining a homeless person who does not have $500 to their name does nothing to solve the problem of their not having a place to live. They'll still be sleeping on a park bench. Much like blaming people for using plastic straws while fossil fuel companies pump trillions of pounds of carbon dioxide into the atmosphere, we've opted into blaming the wrong person. Fines aren't actually fixing homelessness, and plastic straws are not the reason we're in a climate crisis. We default into attacking or blaming individual people for falling into holes inside the system instead of trying to change the system.

Think about this in an environmental context for a moment. You may drive a car every day—that car emits greenhouse gasses. But your car emits nowhere near the emissions that one day of fracking by an oil company does. We know for a fact that 71% of global emissions come from just 100 companies (Griffin 2017). ExxonMobil emits more emissions in one day than even the highest consuming people will emit in their *lives*. But we work ourselves into a frenzy campaigning against plastic straws instead of demanding these companies change their ways. The energy is misdirected, and the misdirect hurts us, the people, and benefits the system.

But the history of humankind has been creating and then changing systems.

COMMERCE VS CAPITALISM

Is all selling and buying an exploitative trap then? Is there any way to pay or get paid that doesn't end in environmental or social disaster?

Yes, and we've been doing it for tens of thousands of years. Trade and commerce are not inherently exploitative systems, and they are fantastic ways to get our needs met in a more equitable way. A common misconception is that simple commerce is the same exact thing as unchecked capitalism.

To put it as simply as possible, commerce is the exchange or trading of goods and services. Commerce has been around since human societies have existed in various forms. Bartering was an early form of commerce;

you have an apple, and I have a cucumber. We trade one apple for one cucumber. Currency developed so people could have a fixed price for an item. Different fruits could be valued differently when it came to doing business, but one copper coin was the same unit of value all the time. With currency in the mix, I could now give you one copper coin in exchange for your apple, regardless of what else I had of value to my name.

Capitalism, on the other hand, is only one way of organizing said commerce, where private individuals own businesses instead of the general public. Capitalism demands ongoing growth, which is a fancy way of saying capitalism needs ever increasing profits to function. And it's that demand for growth that distinguishes capitalism from commerce and that makes capitalism so exploitative. Companies and the owner class are constantly looking for ways to extract more profit while lowering costs. In our present day, that's why you see the push from hiring full-time employees to hiring gig workers with no benefits. This lowers the companies' out-of-pocket costs, because they no longer have to pay out as much in salary or in benefits such as health care for their workers, but they still receive the same value of labor from their gig employees as they do their full-time employees.

Commerce itself is not inherently a bad thing. There's nothing wrong with buying something you need, as long as the power balance of how that thing got made and distributed is not hugely lopsided. Serfdom was lopsided. Enclosure was lopsided. And the shareholder capitalism we are beholden to today is lopsided.

A REMAKING IS POSSIBLE

Chelsea Fagan wanted to work less.

Fagan is the CEO of a successful media company, the Financial Diet, which regularly does over $1 million in revenue and is a big name in the financial education space. But Fagan had come to the conclusion that work was not going to be her main purpose in life. This presented a small challenge in a country where work dominates everything from our waking hours to our conversations. According to the Federal Reserve's 2022 Economic Well-Being of U.S. Households survey, 37% of Americans cannot cover a $400 emergency expense in cash, largely due to rising cost of living expenses (such as housing and transportation). This presents a problem; if people work less, they have even less money. A high cost of living keeps people working, just like capitalism wants.

Fagan wondered how she could work less, continue to earn the same amount, and keep her company afloat amid a challenging media landscape.

She found her answer in a four-day workweek.

"There had been several media stories about larger companies doing it and it working, and I felt like one of the biggest advantages in being a small company is that you can be pretty agile. And so I definitely felt a strong sense of 'if they can do it, we should be able to do it and it's at least worth trying,'" Fagan told me.

In June 2021 the Financial Diet team decided to try a six-month experiment where the 10-person team would work 32 hours a week, four days a week. Fridays would now be part of the weekend, and pay would remain the same. Working fewer hours would not mean taking home fewer dollars at the Financial Diet. Employees also retained their six weeks of paid time off during the experiment.

After six months, the team decided to extend the four-day workweek. After one year, it became a permanent company policy. For Fagan's company, moving down from the 40-hour workweek to the 32-hour workweek brought an increase in business engagement. Overall revenue remained steady, while in 2022, a year into the experiment, the company saw its highest-ever profit margin. The company Instagram page grew by 20%, YouTube subscribers grew 11%, and the newsletter subscriber count doubled. The shorter workweek in no way hindered the company's financial growth.

How much time we spend working is a social norm that we establish. Today's norm is a 40-hour, five-day workweek. That was once unimaginable. When humans were largely agricultural, farmers worked sunup to sundown, or around 70 hours a week, seven days a week. When industry and commerce made their way onto the stage of human history, we changed the work norm and organized a week into work and rest days.

By the 1800s, work had changed yet again, with workers from Wales to the US laboring in industrial factories for anywhere from 10 to 15 hours a day, usually six days a week. Working conditions during the Industrial Revolution were awful. Without workplace protections, many factory workers lost body parts due to using unsafe machines. In textile mills, the majority female workforce worked 12-hour days, six days a week. Women workers used their hands to replace bobbins in industrial looms, a job that came with the risk of losing your hand to the machine. Children also pulled 12-hour shifts; between 1880 and 1910, about one-fourth of all cotton mill workers in the Southern US states were below the age of 16.

It was the efforts of workers' unions during the Industrial Revolution that brought about the international normalization of an eight-hour workday and a five-day workweek. In 1817 Welshman Robert Owens coined the phrase "eight hours' labor, eight hours' recreation, eight hours' rest."

And across the world, the workday began changing once again. Just as we had shifted from sunup to sundown farm days to the 15-hour workdays in factories, we shifted into the then-new eight-hour workday. In 1869, then–US President Ulysses S Grant issued Proclamation 182, which mandated an eight-hour workday for federal government employees. The Mexican Revolution brought forth an eight-hour workday, as well as labor protections for women and children in 1917. Workers' strikes across the United States from the mid-1800s through the early 1900s led to the normalization of the eight-hour workday by the 1930s.

To think of the 40-hour workweek as the sacred key to productivity is simply untrue. As society changes yet again, this time with more technology and machine work than ever before, we have the opportunity for more people to work less than 40 hours a week. We've changed our work system before, and we can change it again.

Despite the 40-hour workweek being hailed as a necessity for the survival of any company (and oftentimes touted as necessary to the survival of the very economy), Fagan's company had found that it was unnecessary to work 40 hours for the business to work well. The decision to work less had made the company *more* financially sustainable, improving focus and morale during work hours. It also improved the personal lives of the employees, who reported that having Fridays off made them feel more valued as a worker, and increased their overall life satisfaction. What could happen to our money and our world if more companies made this choice? If we worked less, would we drive less, and thus lower carbon emissions on a broad scale?

Work has become the defining action of most of our lives. Work is the activity that dominates our waking hours. Increasingly, it is the activity that dominates our thoughts as well; 74% of Americans report being stressed about money. When people don't have enough money, they are likely to work more and longer hours. The basic math of capitalism is that by working more, workers have more income. If being stressed about money begins to cannibalize your free time, working more seems like the obvious solution to both problems.

IT'S ALL JUST AN EXERCISE IN CREATIVITY

Since there has been a mainstream financial culture, there has been a financial counterculture.

Just because a system exists does not make it correct or the best option available. Margaret Thatcher, an English prime minister, is famous for many reasons, one of them for saying, "There is no alternative [to capitalism]." This shows a profound lack of imagination, in my humble opinion. We can't keep doing what we're doing and expect change. We have to make the change happen in the first place, and we can do that by trying out different economic systems. Just because you haven't done something doesn't mean it's impossible to do. I've never completed an Ironman. Doesn't mean hundreds of people don't do that every year.

To define ourselves so narrowly to one system is an insult, and it's quite literally crazy when we can plainly see that that one system is failing.

I work with people one-on-one to create financial strategies and achieve financial goals, and what I always say to people is, "Money is an exercise in creativity."

From budgeting to investing to housing, how we earn, spend, and save our money is an exercise in creativity. Want to build a budget that allows you to eat out every night? You can! It just means not spending in other areas. Want to buy a duplex with your best friend and live on one side and have your best friend live on the other? You can! It just means going through the home-buying process together.

Looking at our capitalistic system, you may think that everything has already been set in stone. There is nothing to be done. That, my friend, is a lack of imagination and creativity speaking. Let's open our minds up and let them run free for a second. How else can we live, spend, work, and operate? What change can we make inside capitalism, and what can we do away with?

What could we do if we entertain the idea that there are other ways? What could we do if we put creativity and imagination at the forefront of our economic decisions, as individuals and as governments?

Anything. *We could do anything.*

In 2021, the US GDP was $23.32 trillion. *GDP* stands for gross domestic product, which measures the value of a country's economic output. Under capitalism, the higher the GDP, the wealthier and (economically) healthier a country is. The US has been the world's largest economy by

GDP since 1890 (Baten 2016). We snatched the crown from the British Empire, largely thanks to a major investment into oil and gas production and terrible labor laws that had people working 15-hour days during the Industrial Revolution.

That's 134 years of being the biggest and baddest economy on the planet. Many people point to this as proof that we cannot change what we're doing. We *must* keep things exactly as they are, or lean even more into capitalism; otherwise, we would lose our crown as the wealthiest place in the world.

But sprinkle some imagination into this conversation. What if we continue to make the same amount of money as a country, but we distribute it differently? Because, as we see, money is not the problem in the US. We can afford to do anything we want. We live the way we live because of how and where we spend our money.

Governments have budgets, the same way you have a budget. Only instead of groceries, rent, and car insurance, governments have categories such as national defense, transportation, and health. In the US, different government departments submit requests for funding themselves every single year. In March 2024, the Department of Defense published a request for an $849.8 billion budget, for one year of funding (US Department of Defense 2024).

Hop in a time machine with me for a second. In 2020, when the Covid-19 pandemic hit the US, parents panicked. Suddenly they couldn't go to work, and their incomes tanked. At the same time, their children still got hungry every day, and the young ones still needed diapers. In a country with no federally subsidized childcare or paid parental leave, parents found themselves falling off the edge of a financial cliff. Parents found themselves balancing work from home, school from home, childcare, and lower income all at once.

In response, the US government did something unusual; it stepped in and provided different forms of direct financial aid to parents.

One, the Child Tax Credit, helped pull over 46% of children out of poverty in 2021 alone. The tax credit was part of the American Rescue

Plan, an economic stimulus plan to help stop the negative economic effects of the pandemic. It increased the normal Child Tax Credit (which is a credit parents can deduct from the amount of money they owe on their taxes) from $2,000 per child to $3,000 per child for children over the age of six and from $2,000 to $3,600 for children under the age of six. It also raised the age limit on children that can be claimed from 16 to 17.

But most crucially for many American parents, the expansion of the credit also included monthly payments of $300 for each child who was five and younger, and $250 for children between the ages of six and 17. That was cold hard cash each month that parents could put toward childcare costs or groceries or the power bill.

Parents who were struggling to work and educate their kids while also staying sane during the shelter-in-place orders and daycare closures found a ray of hope through the opportunities the Child Tax Credit offered. Their lives and work had drastically changed, but *because the government had changed,* they hadn't fallen off that financial cliff.

In total, federal spending on children under 19 years old increased by 15%, or nearly $77 billion, between 2019 and 2020. That was $7,810 per child, and came from a combination of $6,264 in direct spending from federal programs tax credits paid out to families, as well as $1,546 in overall tax reductions for families.

In 2022, the expansion of the Child Tax Credit expired. Families were back on their own—no more direct help or larger tax break from the government. Some Americans supported this, while some were angry that parents were laid out to dry in such a way. But what have I been saying this whole chapter? There is no divine, natural law that we are all beholden to that says, "The Child Tax Credit expansion shall expire in 2022, and nothing shall be done to stop this." Family funding laws are not like gravity.

It is entirely possible to take $77 billion from the Department of Defense and give it to America's parents. We've already done it. We know it works. In one year we pulled nearly *half* of children in the US out of poverty. Imagine if we spent $77 billion per year on our kids for a decade, while still giving the Defense Department $772.8 billion in funding for the year.

To put it more simply, let me quote Cher Horowitz:

> So, OK, like right now, for example, the Haitians need to come to America. But some people are all, "What about the strain on our resources?" But it's like when I had this garden party for my father's birthday, right? I said R.S.V.P. because it was a sit-down dinner. But people came that, like, did not R.S.V.P. So I was, like, totally buggin'. I had to haul ass to the kitchen, redistribute the food, squish in extra place settings; but by the end of the day it was, like, the more the merrier! So if the government could just get to the kitchen, rearrange some things, we could certainly party with the Haitians. And in conclusion, may I please remind you that it does not say R.S.V.P. on the Statue of Liberty. Thank you very much.

The question of changing our money systems here isn't "*Can* we do that?" The question is "*Why aren't we doing it?*"

CHAPTER THREE

SUSTAINABLE SPENDING + RETHINKING CONSUMER CULTURE

The ultimate, hidden truth of the world is that it is something
that we make, and could just as easily make differently.

—David Graeber

The first thing you notice when you exit the Havana airport is the heat. The Caribbean nation is hot and humid. It's also a shining example of sustainable living.

Growing up in the United States, you learn very little about Cuba beyond "Fidel = bad. Communism = bad. Embargo = good." The nuance, even about our own country's major role in Cuban life and politics, just isn't taught. To understand how sustainable living and spending thrives here, we have to understand the big picture of how things do and do not make their way into Cuba.

The US embargo against Cuba is one of the strictest in the world and has been in place for over 50 years. The US doesn't trade with Cuba, but we also prohibit other countries from doing so. Criminal penalties for violating the embargo range from up to 10 years in prison to $1 million in corporate fines, and $250,000 in individual fines; civil penalties can be up to $55,000 per violation.

So if France wanted to sell some cheese to Cuba, the US could impose a million-dollar fine on that cheese company. That leaves Cuba in a bit of a tricky situation, where getting modern basics such as gas, clothing, or even food can become difficult—and it's forced them into radically reimagining consumer culture.

LIVING LIKE A CUBAN

There's no thoughtless ease to consumer culture in Cuba. No "Oh, we're running out of toilet paper. Let me run to Target and pick up enough for the next few months. And while I'm there I'll grab a few T-shirts, some sunscreen, and a bag of chips because we can always use those things eventually."

There's no Target. There might not be any sunscreen. The T-shirts available are international donations, usually from some sort of athletic brand. There's no room in homes to store goods for months. And there's certainly nothing to store for months on end.

When I was in Cuba, I broke my toilet seat on the first night. (At 3 a.m. Very embarrassing to have to explain to my host in broken Spanish the next day.) I offered to pay for it, of course, but my host turned down my money. It didn't matter if I paid for it, he explained. There was no place currently selling toilet seats in Havana. He would have to get on a waitlist and just see if they happened to come in in a few months with some donation shipment.

Cubans face the unique challenge of being the only country in the 21st century forced to live like it's the 19th century. Not because of poverty or lack of opportunity, but because of a decision made in Washington, DC, in 1960. Without a free flow of new goods into the country, the Cuban people can't easily buy brand-new things. So every person approaches the things they own with the mindset of care: "This toilet seat must live for as long as possible, because I do not know when, if ever, I will be able to replace it."

Close your eyes, and picture the streets of Havana. I bet classic American cars come to mind. That's because it's insanely expensive and difficult to get new cars to the island. People don't keep these 1957 Ford Thunderbirds running for the Instagram pictures. They keep them running because there's an almost 0% chance they can ever get a new car if that vintage one breaks down.

Humans shop too much today, and in many parts of the world, there is abundant, almost endless opportunity to shop. You can shop from your phone, from your social media accounts, from your inbox. You can step outside and buy gas, groceries, or movie tickets. But our shopping problem isn't shared equally. The United States has about 5% of the world's population yet consumes a whopping 24% of the world's energy—much of it from manufacturing, shipping, and consuming goods. Maybe you're thinking that means we leave our light bulbs on a little longer. No—all those trips to the mall, the meals out, the 20 pairs of jeans that every influencer owns— that's all energy. It takes energy and resources to create all the things we buy. One American consumes about as much energy as two Japanese citizens and about 307 Tanzanians.

Convenience is a truly American value. A common shared mindset in the US is "I should be able to have what I want, when I want, and that is my right as an American." Companies cater to that, and people pay for it. You can have your dog's nails trimmed and even painted by someone else for a price. You can have your laundry picked up, washed, dried, folded, and returned without you ever needing to leave the house. This level of convenience is tied to our spending habits. The easier it is to spend money, the more likely people are to shop. The easier shopping makes your life, the more likely people are to shop. The two feed into each other.

In May 2019, Amazon announced it would push past two-day delivery for some items and *guarantee same-day* delivery for Prime users. Target already had same-day delivery promises for its RedCard holders, and Walmart announced shortly after that that they would do same-day delivery for a membership fee.

This demand for convenience is driving a consumer culture that is killing us, our money, and our gorgeous, wild planet. With shorter delivery times comes greater greenhouse gas emissions. Delivery vans are barely loaded for one, maybe two deliveries at a time just to meet this same-day delivery expectation.

It's wildly inefficient and unnecessary. In the worst-case scenario, with one delivery per trip, the carbon emissions can be as much as 35 times greater than they would be for a fully loaded delivery van (DePillis 2019).

Amazon claims that most of its same-day deliveries are things such as food, diapers, and detergent (DePillis 2019). These are largely disposable goods, which means we're paying a premium to generate more trash, faster.

Spend two seconds in Cuba, and it's clear that Cubans would be flabbergasted at the idea of same-day delivery of new items that will end up in the trash in just a few weeks. They are masters at repurposing items, and goods in Cuba live for decades at the very least and sometimes even generations.

While sitting at a rooftop restaurant with a view of the Caribbean, a server handed me a record cover from the 1970s. Inside was the bar menu. Cubans can't print new menus at will, and there's nowhere in the city that currently has the ability to laminate paper, so the menus they have need to last as long as possible. The owner had the record covers at his house—they provide the coverage he needs to protect his menus while costing him nothing out of pocket.

As the sun sank past the ocean, the lights flickered on. Electricity is widely available on the island, though it's not stable. Blackouts are common. The lights above my table were diffused by a lampshade made from old plastic blender containers. Instead of whipping up a smoothie, these containers have been flipped upside down and placed around a light bulb to diffuse the light.

I ask how much a new lampshade would cost in my beginner Spanish. The waitress pauses and then shrugs. "I'm not sure . . . it really depends on if it's even in the country. You never know what you might get at the black market. Sometimes there are things and sometimes there aren't. You just wait or you get something else."

You just wait or you get something else. A radical concept in the age of same-day shipping and UberEats.

HOW WE DEVELOPED OUR CONSUMPTION PROBLEM

Part of the American identity is an attitude of access to the world. From the white pioneers who looked at the land where people already lived and thought, "That should be mine" to becoming the country with the highest concentration of billionaires, we Americans are really, *really* into consuming.

And it's killing us. I mean that literally, figuratively, and emotionally. We're using natural resources faster, emitting greenhouse gas emissions faster, and piling up garbage faster than ever before, all to fit a narrative that isn't actually making any of us happier or healthier.

To most Americans, the idea that we should have access to everything is rooted in the idea that limitation is oppressive. Because, as we are all told early and often, our way of life has made us the greatest country on earth. Our freedom and liberty paved the way for our innovation, and our innovation has shaped the world we all live in.

When you have a country that is founded on rich white men saying, "I shouldn't have to pay my taxes," you develop an ethos of individualism. Even though our Founding Fathers weren't roaming the aisles at Target, they were laying the foundation for a mindset that says I should have access to everything I want, and I should have it in a moment's notice.

Take clothing, for example. Here in the United States, clothes were largely made at home up until the late 1800s. In the 1850s some of the first advertisements for "clothing made by machines" began to appear (Thanhauser 2022). People began to buy secondhand around the 1880s, when Jewish Americans sold secondhand clothes from street pushcarts. During the crushing economic crash of the Great Depression, thrift and consignment stores came into the mainstream.

The Industrial Revolution changed the way we work; instead of everything being made by hand, products began to be made by machines. Which in turn meant they could be made faster and cheaper. This resulted in stores being able to sell these products more cheaply, which meant people could buy more items. As machines got better and smarter, and we began using them to make more things, our cultural speed of consumption began to speed up.

In the 1920s and '30s, American advertisers turned their considerable power toward selling people more. More everything: clothes, food, household cleaners, tools. Combine the push for people to spend more with the relative ease of producing more machine-made products, and the first levels of overconsumption are born.

And it made sense! Low-income Americans were able to buy the latest fashions much more easily, and immigrants to the United States found that shopping allowed them to assimilate faster. They could buy American-style clothing, American-style food, and use that to work their way into American culture.

Companies began pouring more money into advertising, and creating more products became easier. When American labor began to be too expensive, companies began outsourcing their employees and manufacturing to cheaper countries. In 1985, for example, AT&T shut down their Shreveport, Louisiana, telephone manufacturer and relocated to Singapore (Markides and Berg 1988).

Business 101 tells us that the cheaper you can make something, the cheaper you can sell it for, and the faster you can sell it. Take this model and apply it to almost everything in your eyeline at the moment: books, clothes, furniture, food; most likely they have all gotten the mass production, offshore treatment.

Which brings us to where we are today. We are all buying our way through life, and it comes with a financial, environmental, and personal cost.

We're filling our homes and lives with more and more items every year. But we will not be able to buy our way out of the climate crisis, no matter how cute that "sustainable swap" home decor TikTok video is.

But the wonderful thing about us is that we can approach anything about our lives in a new way, at any time. We are capable of profound change. And we can use our money to shape the world that we actually want to live in that actually works for all of us.

SHOPPING AS A HOBBY

The idea that you can only feel happiness from opening up your wallet is a capitalist scam.

Here, finish this sentence with me:

I feel my happiest when I am_____

_____.

Did you write down something like "shopping online" or "eating out"? Or did you maybe write down something like "spending time with family" or "bringing my fur baby to the dog park" or "having a glass of wine and watching *Love Is Blind* with my friends"?

There is so much joy and abundance to be had that doesn't come from consuming.

Shopping started becoming a pastime around 1952. After World War II, the American economy was blossoming into the juggernaut we know and love to hate today, and it was beginning to drastically change how households consumed.

Yet until the 1950s, households lived on considerably less than even seems feasible today. Our relationship to spending was different, not necessarily worse.

Getting Comfortable with Different Comforts

I lived in Austin, Texas, for 11 years. I moved with a friend from college for the adventure and for the lack of snow. (Anyone who grew up shoveling snow at 6:30 in the morning before they could ride to school knows the deep yearning to be someplace where winters "aren't really a thing.")

Change was what I needed, and change is what I got. Austin has the distinct honor of being a city that experiences both temperatures well over 100 degrees throughout the summer and high humidity rates. It's disgusting and deeply unfair, especially if you're a curly-haired person like me.

This terrible combo makes air conditioning a necessity. It's not something that's just nice to have; it's not something that only rich folks luxuriate in; it is vital to surviving the year. Summer in Austin starts in May and runs through the end of October. In 2022, it didn't rain in Austin for over

50 days straight. Rivers and swimming holes dry up. There is no relief from the sun, let alone from the heat, save for your precious air conditioner.

The history of air conditioning is an interesting one. The machine was first met with suspicion and disgust, rejected by the elite of the 1940s for being unnecessary and unnatural.

The inventor of air conditioning had to work to get his idea into homes and businesses. The first place to adopt air conditioning in the United States? The very epicenter of capitalism itself: the New York Stock Exchange.

Anyone familiar with the political landscape in the United States today will think what I'm about to share is made up. "Fake news," they will cry, but it is in fact a historical record.

President Richard Nixon, famously a Republican who hated Democrats and orchestrated the Watergate scandal to keep himself in office, was also a political champion for environmental rights. The EPA was founded under his administration, and he urged Americans to conserve their energy use in the name of patriotism during the oil crisis of the 1970s.

In 1973, he gave a national address that specifically called out air conditioning (Nixon 1973):

> How many of you can remember when it was very unusual to have a home air conditioned? And yet this is very common in almost all parts of the nation. As a result, the average American will consume as much energy in the next seven days as most other people in the world will consume in an entire year. We have only 6% of the world's people in America, but we consume over 30% of all the energy in the world. Now our growing demands have bumped up against the limits of available supply.

Can you imagine any right-wing presidential candidate saying anything even remotely similar to this today? Today our two major political parties have become so polarized that those to the right of center can't even look at a tree without first needing to declare climate change a hoax. And we as citizens have become so used to a convenience and comfort-first mindset that really any politician encouraging us to reduce our energy usage in the name of saving money would be murdered in the polls.

It wasn't so long ago that our world was very different from how it is today. We lived without air conditioning set at 68 degrees in every building we entered. We lived without two-day shipping. We did not live the way we do today, and life was still full of fun, joy, and beauty. It wasn't so long ago that we had less stuff and still plenty of happiness. We know that we can live and indeed thrive without consuming the way we are now, *because we've already done it.*

Ask any millennial or Zoomer, and they will likely tell you that eco-anxiety, or climate doom, is on their mind. A lifestyle in which they are not pressed to constantly reach for more, a pace of living that is not constantly held up to be compared to their peers—this is what a lot of us want.

Search "cottagecore" on social media and this yearning becomes visual. Cottagecore describes the return to a way of life where baking, long walks in the forest, long flowy dresses, and spending hours growing your own food dominate the highlight reel. It's a rejection of hustle culture and an embrace of slow living, and it's very popular with younger generations.

We can have it! We can have a simpler, happier life that is better for the earth we all rely on. We get there by changing our social standards of happiness, and we do that by changing our actions.

HOW TO RESHAPE YOUR RELATIONSHIP WITH SPENDING

I didn't go to Target at all for two years. Between July 2014 and December 2016, I didn't go into a single Target in all the land.

This was during my "debt sprint" era. I was laser-focused on paying off my remaining student loans while also being very low-income. I was living at the poverty line for a household of one in my county, and my spending came down to an either-or situation. I could make an extra student loan payment or I could spend $34 at Target, but I couldn't do both. There just wasn't enough money to go around!

So I put myself on a Target ban. And man, I freaking *love* Target. What is it about walking into a Target that soothes the soul? It's bright, there's so many things to look at, and I always feel that if I buy something there, what I'm really walking out with is a better version of myself.

You might imagine that someone who feels so passionately about a soulless corporation that doesn't even know I'm alive might have a hard time not entering a store for two whole years. But I managed to do it anyway. Anything that I was getting at Target I could find at other stores. My grocery store had the face moisturizer and wine that I was buying at Target. Goodwill had the clothes I needed. And to be honest, everything else I was buying from Target was a bunch of stuff that I ended up donating or throwing away within a few months.

I had just been going there weekly on some sort of autopilot because the rest of my life sucked.

In June 2014 I was working basically only on the weekends as a caterer. My weekdays were long and empty. I would apply to jobs online, watch Netflix, have a panic attack that I was going to die under a pile of student loan bills, and then the day would end. I was depressed, I was professionally stuck, and I was pretty damn broke. (Remember, I made $18,000 before taxes in 2014.)

I started going to Target to help the hours pass. I would walk up and down the aisles and convince myself that I did in fact need that wicker basket so that I could finally properly organize my closet. Or I did need that card stock and those new scissors so I could spend my copious free time tapping into my creativity via card-making and scrapbooking. Everything I purchased made sense because I *made it* make sense.

And if you had asked me at the time whether I was an environmentally minded minimalist, I would have answered with a passionate *yes*. Because in my mind, since I was so low-income, and since I didn't eat meat, and since I wasn't flying to vacation destinations each month, I was a minimalist! Never mind that I was slowly emptying the $1 bins at Target and filling my bedroom closet up with $8 clothes that I couldn't even remember buying. Never mind that I was literally trying to buy my way out of depression, searching for personal meaning in the home decor aisle of Target.

My Target ban was life-changing. It showed me how easily I can and will slip into habits that *I don't even want to have.* It showed me that I couldn't find answers to my personal and professional dilemmas in the skincare aisle. And it showed me how stepping back from a weekly shopping habit can be just as easy as starting one, can save me more money, and can rewire my relationship with how I find my joy.

Once I wasn't going to Target anymore to trigger my dopamine, I needed to get that fix somewhere else. I'm a planner by nature, and so I did what people have done for generations. I looked to my community for help. Community! It's everything. Community, friendship, family; this is the pillar we should all be able to lean on. Target doesn't love me back. But my friends do. Target doesn't want to hang out with me. But my friends do.

I leaned into that community to help build a world outside of shopping. But instead of going out for a night of drinking (I was 25, and my hangovers didn't last two days at a time yet), or a day of shopping together, I started putting together free day trips in and around Austin for my friends and I to experience together.

One trip was a two-hour ride south of Austin to Enchanted Rock State Park, a classic Austin experience. Four of my friends and I carpooled down there, splitting gas and the $7 entry fee, and spent the day hiking and eating snacks we'd packed. Another trip was to a free movie night at Auditorium Shores. The movie (*Jurassic Park*) was a free event put on by some nonprofit, and we brought our own blankets, drinks, and snacks to share. Another was an afternoon at my house, watching *Bedknobs and Broomsticks*, an absolutely slept-on classic that is unhinged in the best way. (Seriously: watch it ASAP.)

I also started volunteering at an after-school program for high school girls at risk of dropping out. In the program we worked with the girls to develop self-esteem, friendships, and talked through how to deal with the difficulties of high school romances. Now, instead of spending Monday–Friday alone in my bedroom, ruminating on my student loan debt or in the aisles of Target, I was embracing my values: spending time with the people I love, working on causes I feel passionate about. I wasn't spending money on plastic crap from Target. My consumption level was going down while my joy level was going up.

Changing Consumption Habits

Can we really consume less and still be happy? Where can joy even come from if it doesn't cost money? At first these questions might sound silly and over the top. But the facts are staring us in our faces; today most people are getting their joy by paying for it. From new clothing, to new video games, to dinners out with friends, to paying to join a soccer league, we are spending more and more money each year to enjoy our time on this planet.

And there are more and more places where we can spend money. When my mother was a teenager, Starbucks didn't exist, let alone exist on every third street corner. There was no Amazon, no one-day shipping. There simply were fewer places that people could shop at than there are today.

I've always thought the phrase "cost of living" was dystopian. It could be the title of an Octavia Butler novel. I mean, why does life come with a literal price tag? And the more I tugged at this thread, the more a new phrase burrowed into my brain: "cost of happiness." It rattles around in my head every time I pull out my credit card to spend money in order to have fun. It feels as if every time I want to see friends, or look cute, or have a date night with my partner, it costs money. Free time, fun time, the little pleasures that make life worth it; for many of us, these have become synonymous with *spending money.*

What were the last three friend hangs you attended? For me it's a dance class, a dinner party, and a restaurant dinner. All three of them cost me money. Meaning that I had to pay in order to see my friends.

That's why most of us, if asked to cut back on spending, will balk. We will interpret the question as "Why don't you enjoy your life *less*? See your friends *less*. Look *less* chic."

And it's a fair interpretation. I know that for many people, small purchases have big happiness returns. For the single parent who picks up Starbucks on the way to dropping their kid off for school, that cup of coffee is a warm jolt of caffeine for them, and that muffin they bought for their kid buys them a few moments of silence while it's munched on in the backseat.

Or there are plenty of people who enjoy the lavish options that modern life offers. People want to fly on private jets and have 10-bedroom homes, and they want designer purses and shoes. Some people want to have a closet dedicated solely to their sneaker collection.

What I'm proposing isn't for all of us to give up electricity, move into caves, and start rock collections. Instead, I'm saying that consumption cannot and should not be our only avenue to enjoying our time on this weird and wonderful planet.

Poor people live sustainably. Rich people don't. We know this for a fact because we know that every dollar spent turns into an average of 0.25 kilograms of greenhouse gas emissions (MacKinnon 2021). Therefore, the more money you spend, the more emissions you create. And the less you spend, the less you create.

Don't get me wrong: I don't think there's any nobility in poverty, or that being broke teaches us the meaning of life. Being broke is hard and stressful, and it can literally kill people. In the US, about 900,000 people die from poverty-related issues every year (Brady, Kohler, and Zheng, 2023). Not having money is a death sentence in a country like ours.

But spending our way to happiness just leads to a dead end. I think most of us know that in some way. We've been to bachelor parties that cost us $1,700 for the weekend and thought, "What am I doing here?" We've bought designer shoes and been elated in the store, only to be riddled with financial anxiety when we get home. We've experienced financial anxiety when the credit card bill comes due and we can't even remember what half the purchases were.

"People who save money report better overall well-being, including less psychological distress," Sabrina Helm, study author and associate professor tells CNBC's *Make It*. "And people who buy less and consume less show less depressive symptoms, so there's a positive mental health effect."

Another study shows that when we spend money to buy back time by, say, hiring a house cleaner so that we don't have to spend our weekend hours mopping the floors and can hang out with friends instead, we're happier.

The same study showed that when people do spend repeatedly on material purchases, they're less happy. I'm not knocking the people who get genuine satisfaction out of material things. (I personally love glassware. When I thrift a really cool wine glass, I swear I feel adrenaline shoot through my veins as if I just had won gold at the Olympics.) But these studies, among others, show what I think most of us know deep down: we aren't really enjoying the consumption cycle we're so caught up in. Most of us really, deeply want more time, less stress, and enough money to feel safe. We don't need a closet full of clothes with the tags still on them, or a junk drawer filled with God-knows-what in the kitchen.

We can turn to the secondhand and barter economy to fill our lifestyle needs and desires while also saving money, saving time, and increasing joy. We can opt *out* of certain systems and *into* others.

For example: utilizing the secondhand economy. The "secondhand economy" refers to buying things used: used cars, thrifted clothing, that couch from your neighborhood social media group.

Buying things secondhand *is* better for the planet than buying new. Do you know how to make a new pair of jeans? Jeans largely come from cotton, one of the most water-intensive plants to grow on the whole planet. We also use pesticides and fertilizers to grow cotton, which kill pollinators such as bees, extending the negative environmental impact just to get this cotton out of the ground.

Next is the water usage. One pair of jeans requires about 3,781 gallons of water, start to finish (World Bank 2019). Water is used for dyeing the jeans and distressing the jeans to get them to look stylish.

Finally there's shipping the jeans. Jeans made in Bangladesh but sold in Los Angeles have to travel over 8,022 miles. That's a lot of carbon emissions.

Shopping secondhand (or trading or bartering) for something that you need means this process has to be replicated fewer times. Less water usage. Less dye pollution. Fewer carbon emissions. It's a win all around.

So while we advocate and vote for British Petroleum to stop dumping oil almost directly into the mouths of baby seals, we can also take action in our own lives. We use money every day, right? Combining lowering your consumption levels with changing where you shop is a way that we as individuals can use our money to have an impact on the world around us.

OKAY, SMARTYPANTS, WHERE CAN I FIND THIS JOY YOU'RE HARPING ON?

Let me be your anti-consumption Yoda for a few minutes. Grab a pen or pop open a Word document.

Think about the last time you were deliriously happy. I'm talking full to the brim with satisfaction and delight. What were you doing? Whom were you with? How much did it cost you?

What was the last thing you spent money on? Don't look it up! The point here is to see how connected you are to your daily spending. Was it worth the cost to you?

Make a list of your lifestyle values. A lifestyle value is not necessarily a routine or aesthetic. For example, "fast food" is not a value, even though that can show up a lot in your budget. Your actual value is *convenience.* **You value convenience so that you can spend more time doing something you love.** This is a common value. And it often leads to people overspending in areas *such as* fast food because they don't have to cook or clean up, and thus they have more time.

Write out your financial anxieties. What parts of your financial life are currently stressing you TF out? Identifying these can show us the big-picture lifestyle and money areas to focus on to get the literal most bang for our buck.

Now that we are armed with this information, we are ready for the next step: making some lifestyle changes! Change is beautiful and hard. Every single change I've been through has been a rollercoaster ride, but they've mostly taken me to places that I loved. I think making some lifestyle changes that affect your money, and that are more sustainable for old Mother Nature, will lead you to a place you love.

Remember that *community* is key to sustainability and to seeing financial success! We thrive when we have others to support us. We learn from others, lean on others, and lift up others.

Think about how you spend your free time. List out a few of the activities you've done with loved ones recently:

_____

_____

_____

_____

Now, which of these can you replace with a zero-cost activity? You're still going to see these folks! You're just trying to not spend money while doing it.

I can replace _____ with

_____.

Make a list of things you use in your life that you can start getting used or for free. For example, you can get free books (and audiobooks) from your library and the Libby app. You can get free clothes by joining your local Buy Nothing Group.

_____

_____

_____

_____

Here are some national resources that you can use to participate in the secondhand or trade economy.

Upcycling:

- Freecycle
- Buy Nothing groups
- Buy/swap/trade groups

In the next chapter, we'll talk more about how the power of community can help us all save more and reduce waste.

CHAPTER FOUR

YOUR SUSTAINABLE LIFESTYLE AND THE SOLIDARITY ECONOMY

. . . but because this society is essentially a consumers' society where leisure time is used no longer for self-perfection or acquisition of more social status, but for more and more consumption and more and more entertainment. . .

—Hannah Arendt

I work with people one-on-one to build spending plans, and the question I ask every single one of my clients is: What does financial security mean to you?

I always phrase it like this: "What does financial security look like to you? Is it a number, like 'I need $3 million to my name to feel secure,' or is it more of a lifestyle you see yourself living?"

No one has *ever* told me it's a number. Every single person has responded with an outline of a lifestyle they'd ideally like to live, and after working with hundreds of clients, I've noticed that there are three goals that most people touch on when painting a picture of their financially secure life:

- working less and having more free time with friends and family
- being able to spend without worrying they will go into debt
- being able to explore interests without needing to profit from them

All of which is extremely reasonable! And great news: all these goals are very achievable with sustainable living and a green money strategy. The life that you want to live is found within the world of sustainability, even if you don't want to wear tie-dye or drink hemp milk. We have the chance to redefine wealth from simply a pile of cash in a bank account, or a number on a screen. We can build social wealth, community wealth, time wealth, and design the lifestyle that benefits us and the world most.

FREE CHILDCARE? IN THIS ECONOMY?

Money and a desperate need for help with childcare is what led Elizabeth Doerr to join a babysitting co-op. While cultures around the world have long used joint effort to raise a child, in the US we largely expect parents to be able to "do it all" themselves. From giving birth, to teaching your kids how to tie their shoes, to paying for daycare, American culture overwhelmingly says, "This is the parents' job and the parents' job alone." We have no federally mandated paid parental leave, and no subsidized childcare help for working parents. The average weekly daycare cost in the US in 2024 for one child was $321 (up 13% from $284 in 2022) (Care.com Editorial Staff 2024). That's $15,408 a year, in a country where the median household income was $74,580 in 2022 (US Census Bureau 2022).

For Elizabeth and all parents around the country, a night out is impossible without someone to watch your kids. If you've moved away from family who might do it for free, you need to pony up cash for the privilege of leaving your house. An evening babysitter costs somewhere in the $20–$30 an hour range, adding roughly $90 or more in childcare costs to the cost of date night.

In her babysitting co-op, Elizabeth traded babysitting for childcare hours. Each family in the co-op began with five hours of childcare to trade. When a family wanted someone to babysit, they would coordinate on a spreadsheet the details of the sit: time, date, place, length, number of kids, and details such as "gluten-free home" or "you'll need to pick up child from school." The sit would be chosen by someone who was available at that time, and then the sitter would accrue hours they could "spend" on someone else in the group watching their child in the future. The parents meet quarterly to discuss rules and vote on any structural changes, air out any grievances or hiccups between families, and vote on adding or removing families from the co-op.

It's a rather simple and yet fairly shocking way of approaching childcare in the US. Until I encountered Elizabeth's story, I had never heard of this kind of approach to childcare. All of my parent friends have their kids in daycares, costing them anywhere from $1,200 to $1,800 a month. Elizabeth, on the other hand, would watch a co-op member's child for three hours, and in return, that member would watch her child in the future for the same amount of time, and not a single penny was ever exchanged.

Community was the currency. Community was the true wealth for Elizabeth and her co-op. Without knowing her neighbors, without building personal connections, this co-op would never have existed. Instead, every member of the co-op was able to get some of their childcare needs met without having to spend any money, while also fostering strong bonds with people and families in their neighborhood. Here, neighbors were not people to be afraid of or annoyed by. They were each other's village. Elizabeth would go on to become the godmother to one co-op member's children after knowing each other for five years.

In a small way, the babysitting co-op also helped the entire neighborhood become a little greener. Babysitters didn't have to drive halfway across the city, spewing carbon emissions as they go, to get to Elizabeth's house; they could simply walk over from across the street, or from three houses down.

MONEY IS CREATIVE, ACTUALLY

I always like to say to people that money management is an exercise in creativity. Our current system tells us there is only one way to get your needs met: by buying what you need. You must buy food at the grocery store. You must buy friendship through only seeing your friends at restaurants or bars. You must buy health through paying for a gym membership.

While some of these are of course places you might joyfully spend money, it's the underlying assumption of capitalism that you have to spend money that irks me and that loses us good things such as community while increasing problems such as eco-anxiety. Flexing our creative muscles in our financial lives gives us options outside of simply "spend, spend, spend."

Elizabeth was able to find free childcare through a community babysitting co-op. What can you get from investing your time and energy into community, instead of simply pulling out your wallet?

Maybe a babysitting co-op isn't in your future, but how about a cooking co-op? Let's say Sarah and Pablo make enough vegetarian lasagna and homemade bread for themselves and their neighbors Joe and Melissa to have dinner for two nights this week. In return, Joe and Melissa give Sarah and Pablo two nights' worth of mashed potatoes and pork chops. Each family cooks one meal but eats for four nights.

Or maybe a neighborhood rideshare? Maria owns a car and lends out rides to her neighbors Devon and Dwayne. They in turn complete errands for her, such as picking up her dry cleaning and groceries. One car can meet the needs of three households. Rather than tying yourself down to the "I exchange dollars and cents for all my needs" paradigm of capitalism, you can build micro-communities where you can get your needs met without having to exchange any money. Sprinkle creativity into your life! Use the people around you to build the security that you desire! Make friends with your neighbors!

When Paige Pritchard was 22, she graduated from Texas A&M and got a job that paid for her car, gas, insurance, and cell phone. Her parents welcomed her back to her childhood bedroom and gave her a deal: she could live at home for a year rent free while she worked, began to pay off her $40,000 in student loan debt, and saved up money. It was a perfect deal. She was making about $60,000 a year and had almost no expenses. A year was plenty of time to save up her earnings so she could afford her own apartment and fill her savings account.

And so a year passed. And when her 12 months were up, Paige found herself faced with an uncomfortable truth: she had saved no money. She couldn't move out of her parents' house. She had spent the entire last year shopping. She shopped on her lunch break, to decompress from a stressful morning. She ate almost every single meal out and spent time with friends at expensive happy hours. She had made almost no headway on her student loans and was now staring down the barrel of having to pay for her own rent, utilities, and living expenses while she had nothing in her checking account.

"My story is kind of impulse shopping my way through that entire salary," says Paige. "I didn't have the money in my checking account that

I needed to pay for a security deposit, and my parents were like, 'Well, where did all your money go? Because we know how much you make, and we know you have basically no expenses.'"

By and large, most Americans are in similar positions to 22-year-old Paige. As we mentioned in Chapter 2, 37% of Americans couldn't cover a $400 emergency in cash in 2022 (St. Louis Federal Reserve 2024), and 18% of Americans said the largest nonemergency expense they could cover using only their savings was under $100.

This is a hard way to live, and most Americans state that money is their biggest source of stress. But at the same time, what is the alternative? Rent has to be paid; food's got to be eaten. If we were all Bezos, this savings thing would be less of a problem, but we're not!

As Elizabeth proves, billions in the bank is not the only way to find security, community, and peace. Most humans throughout history have relied on social and community wealth, not monetary wealth, to live full and rich lives.

FOOD SOLIDARITY FOR ALL

Nkoula Badila has grown food in Hudson, New York, Mexico, and Guatemala. What she grows, she eats, and what she doesn't need, she gives away to her neighbors. A passion for cultivating land was instilled in her by her West African father, who taught her and her nine siblings how to plant, tend, and harvest in their own backyard. In 2020, when Covid forever changed the world, Badila's food growing skills were thrown into sharp relief. The entire global food chain had been upended by the new virus. Grocery stores around the US were experiencing shortages of food as well as items such as toilet paper.

For Badila, growing food was no longer a hobby or a family tradition her father had instilled in her and her siblings. It was a vital skill that she had that could feed herself and her community. All she had to do was spread the knowledge. So in the middle of a global meltdown, Grow Black Hudson was born.

Grow Black Hudson helps people in the Hudson, New York, area turn their yards into food gardens. In Badila's eyes, most people have been severed from their connection to the land they walk every day and from one another. Grow Black Hudson started at a time of literal separation and where social and political differences were driving people further and further apart. Badila saw this as a continuation of the separation that people have from nature. People don't know what can be grown around them, and they don't know how to nurture plants. People aren't connecting with one another or the land in a way that moves both parties forward. With the rise of social isolation in general, and the specific six feet social distance Covid required for safety, Badila wanted to use food and gardening as a way for people to reconnect with each other and the land.

"I feel like there's a lot of segregation and in a lot of different kinds of ways and just kind of even the way people grow up and it's like, 'I'll take care of myself or my family.' There's a lot of this kind of subtle segregation that's widespread, where people are very closed off about ways that they can help each other," Badila tells me over the phone. She's talking about that feeling many of us feel, the loss of "the village."

Seven of her siblings moved back to Hudson as adults, and Badila lived with several of them in her childhood home in 2020. Sharing food, bathrooms, and the television is Badila's norm, established in her by her parents. The connection she shares between all her siblings is the connection she hoped to bring to her greater community during 2020. "I feel like coming from a Congolese background, my family incorporates a lot of different community aspects, like free community-accessible activities that are just great for building that network, through theater or through our dancing, our drumming, our music," Badila says.

Since 2020, Badila has started a Grow Black Hudson Instagram and Facebook page. This is how people find her now, and how she has extended the reach of her work.

People will send a Facebook message to Badila, and she will show up to their home, dressed in overalls and with garden tools in hand. Together, over weeks, they will till the soil, discuss which plants make sense for the amount of light the yard gets, and step-by-step, transform the yard into a functioning garden.

Badila makes almost no money from this work. These hours spent in strangers' front lawns, the labor put into digging, weeding, and watering, none of it is paid. The money isn't the point. Community resilience is the point. People getting fed is the point. Building strong relationships is the point.

For four years she has planted gardens all around Hudson, and she says the work continues. Today, she has more support from the food community near her. Local organic farms donate different materials to her, such as native plant seeds and soil, which she uses in the community yard gardens. People whom she helped create a garden last year donate back tools or the fruits of their garden, and Badila passes them on to the next person who wants to build something new. In some ways, she's a one-woman show, but viewed through a different lens, Badila runs a food-focused, community-focused mutual aid group.

Both Badila and Doerr were able to meet a need without money via their community connections. Neighbors weren't people to be feared but people to embrace and to work with. These connections helped them save money and build social connections that helped them and the people they worked with operate outside of the "buy everything" drone of capitalism.

HOW YOU CAN BEAT IMPULSIVE, ASPIRATIONAL, OR UNNECESSARY SPENDING

When Paige looked at her empty bank account and her full closet, a thought crystallized for her. "What I'm being sold isn't what I thought I was buying," said Paige. Paige had compulsively shopped her way through about $40,000 in one year, and she wasn't happier, smarter, or richer for it.

In a world where we see ads at the gas station, on TV, listen to ads on the radio, are inundated with ads on social media, and see ads on billboards and buildings when we leave our homes, we forget that the sustainable choice is often the choice that saves us the most money. A world of constant advertising is a world where we are constantly being conditioned to spend money.

So can we blame ourselves or others for shopping? No. Not even a little bit. But this isn't about blaming someone. It's about recognizing that the game is rigged and finding a way out. The first step to building a sustainable money plan is recognizing the types of spending you're participating in.

Aspirational Spending

Paige found her way out of the endless consumption matrix by realizing that she was shopping for someone that she wasn't.

Aspirational spending is when we spend money in pursuit of a person we want to be at some point in the future. We want to become a runner, so we spend $90 on new Nikes, $100 on new Lululemon leggings, and download Simone Biles playlist on Spotify. We think that the purchases will turn us into a runner, instead of, you know, *running*.

"For me, what the biggest shift has been is giving myself the proof before making the purchase," Paige said. "Whenever we want to evolve into a new version of ourselves, whether it's a more organized version of ourselves or a more creative version of ourselves, the first question we ask ourselves is, 'What do I need? What do I need to buy, what gear do I need, what apparel do I need?'"

If you want to become a runner, instead of hopping online and seeing whether Adidas has a women's size 7 sneaker on sale, look toward your calendar, and ask yourself: When, where, and how often?

When will you run? When do you have the free time to do this new activity?

Where will you run? Are you already paying for a gym membership, and you'll become a treadmill person? Or do you want to run through the park near your work?

How often will you run? Mark on your calendar how many days in the week you'll go for a run.

All of these questions are much more important to answer to become a runner. Most middle-class people in the US have some kind of footwear they can start walking or running in today, without needing to buy something new. What's usually missing from their identity as a runner is the lifestyle structure to actually complete the run.

As Paige explained, "What I commonly hear from people is, 'Buying things is what will motivate me to start. Once I know I've gone and spent all this money, I'll be ready to start.' And that's a big lie we tell ourselves because it's more of a justification. Because what we have to remind ourselves first is where identity comes from. Identity mostly comes, first and foremost, from our thoughts and beliefs, which will then kind of fuel the actions that we take. What's going to give you the identity of a runner, of someone who takes care of their health in this way, is you actually going out and running."

Commit to creating a walking habit for two weeks before you purchase any running gear. If you can make it out of the house three times a week for two weeks consistently, that's the proof that you can devote the time to running. With that proof, you can then shop for the items you need to make running a part of your lifestyle.

Impulse Spending

Ever wonder why grocery stores keep candy right next to the checkout area? It's because stores know that making you stare at chocolate-covered deliciousness while you wait to pay will weaken your spending muscle and strengthen your impulsiveness. If you have to walk by something, or stand next to it for a period of time, you're more likely to buy it.

In fact, research has shown that impulse spending makes up 60% of all purchases (Inman and Winer 1998, Mattila and Wirtz 2008). Our brains are really incredibly advanced and incredibly basic at the same time; we see something we know we like, and we want it at that moment. Stores know this, and they design their entire layouts around it. That's also why you have to walk to the back of most grocery stores to find the basics such as milk and eggs, forcing you to walk past the Pop-Tarts and the seasonal candy displays on both your way back there and then back up to the front.

Impulse spending is a habit many of us find hard to break, so approach this money change with compassion for yourself. You're not a financial disaster if you get a Butterfingers on the way out of the grocery store! But many Americans in particular justify impulse shopping as "it makes me happy" or "I deserve this treat." We allow the short-term desire to overrun our other, usually deeper, desires. With the rise of one-click shopping from social media apps and websites, it's easier than ever to let our impulses guide our overall shopping habits.

Try reconfiguring your thought process from thinking, "I deserve this Butterfingers" to "I deserve a healthy planet, healthy body, and a debt-free life." What actions are in pursuit of those goals? Is it really buying the Butterfinger, or that seventh pair of $100 Lululemon leggings? Aligning your actions with your deepest-held desires provides you a port in the overconsumption storm. Use visual reminders to trigger those deep desires when you're out and about. I changed my phone screen to a picture of my dream house when I began saving for a home of my own. I, like a lot of people, check my phone approximately 2,000 times a day. Seeing that house repeatedly throughout the day did wonders for curbing my impulse shopping. It constantly reminded my brain "Oh, right, *this house* is what I really want, not that $60 shirt I only kind of like."

Paige describes learning to beat impulse spending by saying we've "forgotten how good waiting can feel." Delayed gratification can actually bring us joy, especially when the payoff is something that we deeply desire.

I consumed in the ways that I thought were going to make me happy—but they didn't. We get socialized again with more influencers and ads, and we forget that lesson really quickly.

Try practicing delayed gratification in one area of your spending. See how it feels to curb your impulse spending in this area. Do you find yourself more or less fulfilled when you do actually buy something? Do you feel less distracted in general? Do you feel more or less of a compulsion to spend money every day? Changing our relationship with spending means tuning into how we feel both when we do and do not spend, and when we change a long-held habit.

Random Spending

Sometimes, we just spend money. I mean, I feel as if just walking out of the house costs me $65, and I'm not even sure where it goes most of the time! This random spending is a huge problem that many people want to change about their finances but struggle with exactly because it's so random. People don't know what they're going to spend until they are spending it. How do you budget for the unknown?

The single most helpful spending habit you can start to develop in yourself is to do a weekly review of your spending. Log into your credit card, your debit card, and any apps such as CashApp, Venmo, or Zelle, and grab copies of your spending for the last week. Dump this information into a spreadsheet, or print out copies from each company. Go through, line by line, and highlight your spending into two colors:

- Green for "necessary, keeps me alive and working" spending. These are things such as rent/mortgages, health care, daycare, prescriptions, transportation, and groceries.
- Blue for "nonessential" spending. These are things such as going out to eat, concert tickets, new clothes, and in-app purchases. Basically, all the things you like but don't necessarily require to live.

Here we now have a map of your spending. What does it tell you? Does one color pop up more than the other? Is there one category of spending that pops up over and over? What emotions do you feel looking at this: happiness, shame, confusion, embarrassment?

When I first did this exercise, Target came up as my most repeated purchase. I was going to Target multiple times a week to just wander around, and I always left with something. Sometimes it was just a $5 new notebook, and sometimes it was $56 of stuff I couldn't even recall buying. I was embarrassed that I was buying so much junk at Target, especially because the first time I did this, I was broke as a joke. I was crying myself to sleep at night because of my student loan debt, and I was spending money at Target like it was going out of style? Insert "congrats, you played yourself" meme.

Remember, we're reviewing our spending with compassion for ourselves. We make decisions with the best information we have at the time, in a world that is constantly trying to separate us from our money. We want to build your sustainable spending plan from a place of clarity, self-compassion, and resolve, not from a place of self-loathing.

When I spoke to Paige about her money journey, I asked her what she felt overspending took from her. Had her shopping robbed her of anything? Her answer may resonate with you.

"I really feel that it just took optionality from me. I feel like it took options from me. And. . . it just took so much of my freedom away, which is ironic, because I feel [. . .] with a lot of people, with their spending habits, a lot of people view being able to spend all of your money on whatever you want, whenever you want, I think a lot of people associate that with freedom. What I kind of came to find through that experience is that's actually the opposite of freedom. Because like that one specific situation, it was [. . .] the thing that I really wanted most, much more than all the stuff that I bought, much more than all the clothes and shoes. . . What I wanted much more than that was to be able to move out of my parents' house to be on my own again to regain that sense of freedom that I had kind of gained four years in college. And so I really felt [that] I took that from myself, with my shopping and my consumption habits, so that was my wake-up moment."

INCORPORATE CREATIVITY INTO YOUR FINANCIAL LIFESTYLE

In 2013, Rebecca Rockefeller and Liesl Clark founded a group called "Buy Nothing," which encouraged people in close proximity to one another to gift consumer goods or services to their neighbors. Got a bunch of cloth taking up space in your hall closet? On Buy Nothing, you can gift that to someone in your Zip code who wants to learn how to make their own dress.

This is the gifting economy, a type of economy that has been around for thousands of years but that is largely lost under capitalism. In many cultures around the world, gifting was used as a means of trade to obtain needed items but also as a way of building trust between people.

In Indigenous groups of the Pacific Northwest of the US and Canada, there's a tradition called a potlatch. Potlatches are ceremonies and parties in one, where leaders of the community give away certain items or amounts of wealth to the community.

In the Trobriand Islands, the tradition of gifting Kula rings goes back thousands of years. Different groups of people would travel sometimes hundreds of sea miles to meet with other people and gift them jewelry, including the Kula rings and necklaces. The rings were not, and are not, particularly valuable; the point of the gift was to build trust and good relations between different groups of people. The rings and necklaces were given freely, with no expectation of something received in return. This was not a trade—it was a gift.

Today, in Western societies we have forms of gifting economies within nuclear families. Consider a grandparent paying for their grandchild's college tuition. It's a gift from the family member who has more than they need to the family member who is just beginning their adulthood. Christians commonly tithe part of their income to their churches, a gift given freely in the name of their spiritual beliefs. Even open-source software is part of the gifting economy, where one developer has created something and given it to the Internet at large for anyone else to take, use, and even expand on without the expectation of payment.

The gift economy also exists in nature. As Robin Wall Kimmerer writes in her book *Braiding Sweetgrass*, "That is the fundamental nature of gifts; they move, and their value increases with their passage. The fields made a gift of berries to us, and we made a gift of them to our father. This is hard to grasp for societies steeped in notions of private property, where others are, by definition, excluded from sharing. Practices such as posting land against trespass, for example, are expected and accepted in a property economy but are unacceptable in an economy where land is seen as a gift for all."

Gifts are given with no expectation of anything in return, a hard notion to grasp in a world that feels increasingly fragile and tenuous. For many of us with bills that keep increasing and rights being stripped away, it can feel vulnerable to give a gift and not expect something in return. But in a financial system that seeks to always separate you from your money and from others, the gifting economy can be a way to reconnect with other people while meeting your needs. Kimmerer puts it more eloquently than I can in *Braiding Sweetgrass*: "In the gift economy, gifts are not free. The essence of a gift is that it creates a set of relationships. The currency of a gift economy is, at its root, reciprocity."

In our buy-first world, lots of us end up with things we don't need or ever end up using. Take a look around your house right now; I'll bet you can see one to five things you haven't used in the last month.

Living with such a plethora of things around us opens us to the trade economy quite nicely. Instead of buying those sneakers to develop your running habit, or waiting until a pair in your size comes up on a gifting platform, you can trade for what you need. Take that dutch oven you've never used from your kitchen cabinets, hop on Facebook or Craigslist or a community forum and say, "I have this dutch oven, and I'm looking for a pair of new running sneakers, size seven. Anyone want to trade?"

You'll have gotten rid of something you don't use and brought in something you truly want, all for free. You'll have engaged in your community and potentially met someone new who lives nearby. You'll have kept waste from a landfill and freed up space in your kitchen cabinets. All of these things are green money practices that benefit our wallets and our world.

Exercises

Reflect back on two times that you bought things in pursuit of a new identity. Write down what your real goal was and what about yourself you were trying to change. (For example: you bought free weights and running shoes because you wanted to get stronger. Your goal was to be able to run a half marathon.)

_____

_____

_____

_____

_____

_____

If you're at home, look around yourself right now. How many items can you see that you don't use on a regular basis?

_____

_____

Take 10 minutes and find at least two places that you can give or receive items for free. Check out Freecycle, Buy Nothing, type "swap meets/groups" into Facebook, and look for local community or religious centers.

_____

_____

Commit to a no-spend day once per month. To start, define *no spend* as no eating out, no gifts for yourself or others, no drinks out, and no online shopping. Reflect on how not being able to spend affected your day: Did you notice it? Was it hard, easy, something in between? Did you save money?

_____

_____

_____

_____

CHAPTER FIVE

HOW TO BUILD YOURSELF A SOUP SWAP

When I give food to the poor, they call me a saint. When I ask why the poor have no food, they call me a communist.
—Dom Helder Camara

July 2023 was the hottest month on record globally and likely the hottest month humans have ever lived through (UN 2023). Temperatures reached 53 °C (128 °F) in Death Valley, California, and Santorini, Greece, hit 41 °C (106 °F). In Arizona, the pavement got so hot that if you touched it, you burned yourself. Raise your hand if you feel like collapsing into bed when you think about what climate change is actually going to do to our lives if we don't get out butts in gear.

Well, hello there. Fancy seeing you collapsed on this mattress too!

According to the love of my life, Wikipedia, eco-anxiety is "the generalized sense that the ecological foundations of existence are in the process of collapse." Which . . . yeah!

It's the general sense of doom about our future and how no one seems to give a real fuck, and how every time an absolutely horrifying report about the environment comes out people still expect you to send emails and go grocery shopping, and you feel like the crazy one because you're asking, "Um, hi, what is the *plan here*?"

Eco-anxiety is rational. It is a completely justified and normal reaction to the times we live in. And it is very common. You are not alone in feeling it, and it's exactly the fact that so many of us are freaked the F out about it that is our super-power to change it.

Eco-anxiety can display in many different ways. It can look like:

- depression over the animals and land that have been lost;
- high anxiety when using something such as single-use plastic;
- anger or frustration toward people who don't make the same environmental choices you do or who ignore that climate change is a reality;
- grief over environmental damage; or
- obsessing over personal choices, such as having to use a gas-powered car to get to work.

Social media and global news may also heighten eco-anxiety. In 2022, catastrophic flooding led to a third of Pakistan being underwater for weeks. People around the world watched images of houses being swept away by flood waters. Pakistan's Federal Minister for Climate Change Sherry Rehman took to Twitter to share the devastation, writing, "The crops are gone, lives ruined, livelihoods wiped out, roads swept away, houses destroyed or barely standing . . . Where to pump/drain the water? There's water everywhere."

We watch climate disasters play out in real time from our phones and computer screens. It feels that it is only a matter of time until some such disaster reaches our own lives, and we feel helpless in the face of this inevitability. This is what eco-anxiety wants from us: paralysis in the face of challenges.

However, the reality and brighter truth is that right now, millions of people are working on solutions to our climate problems. And you can be one of them. While in a 2021 Pew Center study, 72% of people from 17 advanced economies in Europe, Asia, and North America said that they expected global climate change to harm them personally at some point, the same study showed that 80% of respondents were willing to make changes to how they lived and worked to reduce the harm of climate change (Bell et al. 2021).

We can overcome eco-anxiety and take action in our own lives to mitigate climate change, and we can do that through our big-picture money decisions (see Chapters 3, 4, 6, 7, 8, and 9!) as well as our smaller daily decisions. A look back through history tells us that our actions will be more successful if we do them together.

STRONGER TOGETHER

Erin Axelrod sits down for dinner with her household every night. That's her one-year-old daughter, her partner, and two other families. Living in the Bay Area is pricey, with San Francisco clocking in at the fourth most expensive city in the entire US. Sharing housing, as well as household duties, saves Erin money, time, and energy.

It also builds Erin's community and allows her to live her values. Erin works at LiftEconomy, an impact consulting firm that works toward an economy that excludes extractive and harmful policies, and includes regenerative and locally independent communities. Basically, Erin's day job is saving the world from the dark side of individualistic capitalism.

So it should come as no surprise that collectivism guides most of the choices in her personal life as well. After growing up in Sonoma County, Erin moved closer into the SF Bay area. When she first arrived in 2014, she made a commitment to spend no more than $750 a month on rent. A tall order in one of the most expensive areas of the US, even a decade ago.

But Erin has succeeded in that mission, and community has been the secret ingredient in her success.

"That [number] was just partly out of necessity," says Erin via Zoom, "and partly because I didn't want to have to compromise my values and have to . . . only look at my clients as something where I had to make a ton of money from my clients every month just to pay rent. I wanted to be able to work with, you know, good nonprofits and folks that couldn't pay huge, huge consulting rates."

At the time, Erin worked helping people installing gray-water systems and reducing their water use in drought-stricken California. (Gray water is water that has been used domestically, commercially, or industrially that doesn't contain serious contaminants and is repurposed. Think about collecting the water from your shower and using it to wash your car.) Repurposing gray water from household items such as washing machines is a great way to lower overall water use and can save people money while lessening the drawdown on community reservoirs.

As you might imagine, a regenerative landscape expert is not always a high-paying job.

"So that decade that I spent, I had to get really creative," Erin explains. "I bartered for housing on a land restoration project. I slept on my best friend's couch for, you know, six months to a year and shared in her rent. I stayed on a houseboat and reduced my rent that way. And then I stayed in another collective (living) house."

Erin leaned into her community to provide her housing that stayed under her $750 a month limit, and in return she gave her community her skills and time. When she bartered for housing on the land restoration project, Erin paid around $200 a month in rent, a number that feels like it's from 1924, not 2014. In exchange for her deeply reduced rent, Erin provided business consulting for the grass-fed meat company that owned the land. (Her best friend and roommate at the time managed the cows via regenerative grazing practices.)

During the year she spent on a friend's couch, Erin contributed $300 a month to rent.

"It was a one-bedroom with an open floor plan kitchen/living room, and I slept on the couch in the living room. I would tuck away my bedroll each morning and bring it out each night. She (my roommate) taught piano out of the main living room. My contributions helped her reduce her rent costs and keep costs down for her piano students," Erin said.

This exchange of effort and time spent in community meant two major things for Erin: she saved money for her future, and she learned how to live with others in a variety of housing situations. By experimenting with what worked for her money and her lifestyle, Erin was able to live at or under her $750 a month limit. Creativity was her ally, and today, Erin can live part-time in her collective housing in harmony, and part-time in a tiny house that she was able to build completely debt free from her and her partner's savings.

THE ANTI-ANXIETY COCKTAIL: ONE PART MONEY, ONE PART TIME, TWO PARTS PEOPLE

The curious truth of the common definition of a successful American lifestyle is that it is often a lonely one. Financial advancement usually means moving away from other people, quite literally. When we are in our early careers, people often live with roommates. As we do things such as pay off debt or earn more, we can afford to live without other people helping to share the rent, and so we move into apartments on our own, or perhaps with our romantic partner only.

People who earn more money tend to move away from apartment living, where we see other people in the hallways that connect our apartments or in the joint mail room, to single-family housing, where you may have a half-acre lawn that distances you from the closest neighbor. Lower-income people may rely on public transportation such as buses or subways, traveling together with hundreds of other people to work or play. A higher amount of disposable income allows people to purchase cars where they can sit alone, darting around the bus that carries their fellow townsfolk.

Consider that the wealthiest among us live behind gates, on estates that often have a literal acreage of land. They fly in private jets with just their inner circle. They can buy out entire restaurants, ensuring they have total privacy for their four-course meal. They attend exclusive parties, where the only other guests have similar net worths.

Money can literally separate us from each other. "Economic resources don't just determine whether families can afford to go on vacation or attend elite schools; they shape how family members depend on one another," writes Stephanie H. Murray in an article entitled "How Affluence Pulls People Away from Their Families" (2022).

This lifestyle is collectively agreed upon to be the norm; it's what you should want and are likely pursuing. However, going it alone may present a strain on your finances as well as your socializing. The $2,000 rent you once shared with three people is now something you need to cover entirely on your own, cutting down how much you can save. Those two other roommates may have been both built-in socializing, catching up in the kitchen after a day of work while making dinner, and a way of learning how to adapt to others' needs. Our social skills grow and strengthen when we meet people who live and think differently from us, and we develop the ability to compromise. Moving away from others means fewer opportunities to do that, which can lead to inflexibility at best and indoctrination at worst.

Financial anxiety is also ruining a lot of our social bonds. Millennials and Gen Z are much more likely to change jobs every few years in search of higher pay, meaning people are moving around a lot. Ever-increasing housing costs cause people to move in pursuit of affordable rent, making it hard to get to know your neighbors over time.

When looked at through the lens of eco-anxiety, this forced separateness might mean that if you're alone in your one-bedroom apartment, freaking out that the entire American West will run out of water, you don't have anyone to talk you off the ledge. You don't have anyone to turn to and say, "Can we do anything about this? Is there anyone else already working on this problem that we can support?" You are left to ruminate in the fear, in the isolation, and the negative feelings can grow.

Simply hanging out more can help us be happier, healthier, more financially stable, and create a more climate-stable planet. Are the friends we make along the way *really* the answer to our planet's woes?

WHAT "IT TAKES A VILLAGE" REALLY MEANS

"It takes a village" is the anthem of parenthood. Tell someone that you feel overwhelmed by the idea of feeding and clothing a child daily, on top of teaching them how to walk, talk, and you know, how to be a good and moral person in this wacky world, and people will smile and tell you, "Well, it takes a village."

Only, most people today, parents or not, feel that they have no village. Continuing a trend born out of the Industrial Revolution, most US-based jobs have been created in major cities in the last several decades. That forces people to live in the most expensive areas of the country, whether or not their family lives there and whether or not they want to. Rising living costs means that most households need two adults working to cover all the bills, reducing the people available to fill the role that women played in decades past as unpaid community builders and homemakers.

It leads me to think of college. For many Americans, college is the only time we live together with people across different racial and economic divides. It's the only time we have regular communal meals with people that are not blood relatives. It's the only time we live within walking distance of everyone we regularly socialize with. According to a 2023 report, "Walkable downtowns, town centers, and neighborhoods comprise only 1.2 percent of metropolitan land area—and 0.07 percent of total US land area—yet they generate 20 percent of the nation's gross domestic product" (Rodriguez and Leinberger 2023). Proximity is better for us and our money, but in the US, we are largely separated by roads, highways, and housing divisions.

College campuses are generally built with the intention to provide both private and community space (dorm rooms and dining halls) and access to any service that people could need (health center, gym, class, and places to get food are all included on most campuses), in walking or biking distance, and usually in close proximity to some kind of public transit. And perhaps most crucially, college campuses are places you can exist without needing to spend money on the day-to-day. You can spend all day on a college campus and have a place to sit, eat, and work out, without needing to open your wallet to do so.

(Sidenote: it kills me when people say we don't need college anymore. College teaches critical skills that are being lost in today's world, notably critical thinking, media literacy, and the ability to be around other people who are different from us! College may be more important than ever before! Okay, tiny rant over now.)

Americans are deep in the loneliness and sadness trenches. We have a full-blown loneliness epidemic, with roughly half of US adults reporting they feel lonely regularly. Loneliness has measurable health and financial impacts too. According to a 2023 report from the US Surgeon General's office, "Loneliness and social isolation increase the risk for premature death by 26% and 29% respectively. Social isolation among older adults alone accounts for an estimated $6.7 billion in excess Medicare spending annually, largely due to increased hospital and nursing facility spending. In the U.S., stress-related absenteeism attributed to loneliness costs employers an estimated $154 billion annually" (Murthy 2023).

Technology has also robbed many of us of the small interactions that were once daily norms—headphones on the subway or at the gym mean we don't approach one another in public places. Work from home has eliminated "water-cooler chats," or the smalltalk that helped make work a way to create friendships. We scroll on our phones while waiting in line at Trader Joe's or the bank instead of commenting to each other on the killer sale this week, or how cute someone's coat may be. Car-centric cities lack walkable areas, forcing us to be indoors or tucked away in cars, often by ourselves.

Without these small social touchpoints, and without a strong in-person social network to lean on for help with things such as childcare, cooking together, or simply sharing a drink at the end of the day, we have lost our villages.

Now layer in the always-present, ever-growing sense of doom around our planet's future. According to a 2021 study that interviewed 10,000 people between the ages of 16 and 25 from 10 different countries, 75% of young people globally think the "future is frightening" due to climate change. More than 50% reported feeling each of the following emotions: sad, anxious, angry, powerless, helpless, and guilty when asked to describe how they felt about climate change. Perhaps most importantly, though, respondents felt *betrayed* by the actions their governments had taken so far on climate change. They felt their futures had been traded for present-day profits (Hickman et al. 2022).

Eco-anxiety leads to a doomer mindset. "Doomerism" is a term born out of the Internet, mostly used to describe someone who is nihilistic around large-scale problems such as climate change or international relations. Our social isolation makes this mindset worse, and many people struggle to see a light at the end of the tunnel when it comes to our global challenges.

Think back to Erin: when she had a financial need, she worked with others to find a communal solution that worked for her *and* for the other person *and* the planet. While not everyone can or wants to work on a regenerative land restoration project, the base of Erin's approach is replicable.

Let's break down Erin's approach step-by-step:

1. She set a financial limit for a specific need: no more than $750 a month on rent.
2. She analyzed her skill set to find a skill she could offer others in trade.
3. She organized her housing search along her environmental values, looking into places that had available housing that were working on environmental projects.
4. She was flexible in what housing could look like for herself.

Do you need to sleep on a friend's couch to reduce your eco-anxiety or save money? No! But can you take these steps and apply them to a financial area of your life to make some changes? Of course!

As a green money nerd, when I moved to North Carolina and found myself without a single friend, I thought, "What am I trying to find in friendship? Do I just want to yell at the next person who walks by, 'HEY, do you want to be friends?' Or do I want to immerse myself in specific communities that align with the things I want in life?" The answer, of course, was the latter.

In my 20s I had built friendships with basically whoever was around. My fellow waitresses at the restaurants I worked in, the women I met at women-in-business events, or the people whom my roommates brought over for movie night. I didn't really approach building my village with thought or care. And while I was lucky in that I did create some friendships that

I still cherish, I also spent a lot of time with people whom I didn't actually have anything in common with. I had a few friend breakups because we were too different to forge a strong and lasting bond.

When I landed in North Carolina I listed out the habits and hobbies I had that I loved and wanted to share with people. For me that was reading, sustainable living, city planning, and walking.

That list led to my next step: *find the people already doing that*. There's no need to reinvent the wheel when it comes to building community; in most places, there are already people doing things you like! Through the power of Google and Facebook, I found a walking club that met four times a month. I decided to host book swaps in public parks around the city, and I found several Facebook groups where I could promote my events for free. I found three sustainability nonprofits and signed up to volunteer with them.

At all three types of events, I was meeting people I was intentionally seeking out, not just random people. I was meeting people invested in the same things I was. And this meant they would continue to show up around that topic! It felt like a cheat code: I already had buy-in from them. I didn't have to convince them to care about the topic—or *me*, by extension. These were people who already liked walking, reading, and sustainability and clearly felt comfortable taking their free time to engage with others around those topics.

But meeting people is only step one in village building. How many times have you met someone, felt you connected, and never seen them again? Without a follow-up, the friendship that could blossom might die on the vine.

The next step is where most people struggle the most: show up repeatedly. I went to the walking club maybe seven times before I met someone whom I really resonated with. From the walking club, we were able to set up a weekly walk of our own, every Thursday afternoon at 4 p.m. I went to probably 10 sustainable volunteering events and met one friend I see and talk to outside the nonprofit. I hosted four book swaps over summer 2023 in parks and spent my 2024 Galentine's Day with two women who came out to one in August.

Over months, I poured time into these people *and* these topics, and I found that people were excited and willing to pour back. But there needs to be buy-in, value alignment, and clarity. I was clear: I'm looking for *friends*. And I'm willing to show up if you are as well.

This is how we build a village in a world that feels increasingly separated and anxiety filled. Much like Erin, I approached meeting my friend needs with a plan.

1. Make a list of the hobbies I had that I was interested in doing more of and meeting people in
2. Research who was already doing things around these topics
3. Attend events repeatedly to build familiarity with people
4. Reach out to people on my own to deepen our connection
5. Keep showing up over time

HOW HELPING MOVE A COUCH SAVED US MONEY AND BROUGHT US SOUP

It was 10 p.m. on a Sunday in July, and there was a loud *thunk* coming from outside our front door. My partner and I had just moved into a new apartment a week earlier, and I was trying to put together our gallery wall in the living room. The *thunk* kept happening, and finally my partner poked his head out our front door. Turns out another young couple were moving into the apartment upstairs, and they were struggling to get their couch up the stairs. My partner put on his sneakers and helped them get the couch upstairs and into their apartment. About 20 minutes after he had first opened the door he was back in our apartment and our new neighbors had their couch securely in theirs.

Two weeks later someone knocked on our door around 8 p.m. I opened the door to find a couple I'd never seen before, offering us a box of macarons with a thank-you note. It was the couch neighbors, coming to thank my partner for his moving efforts. These cookies were the first in a series of exchanges we'd have with our new friends over the next year. When they needed a wine opener, they texted us, asking to borrow ours. When we had a cantaloupe and were going out of town before we could eat it, I gave it to them.

Most adorably, my partner and the woman in the neighboring couple started an impromptu soup swap. Meal prepping is a way of life in my household, but my partner has a knack for making enough food for a family of five instead of our actual two-person home. He packed up some of his vegetable medley and offered it to our upstairs friends; they happily accepted. A week later, we were the recipients of a lentil tomato soup. Over the course of the next few weeks as the season changed from winter to spring, we exchanged soups several more times. A creamy vegan butternut squash soup, a chunky potato soup, and a five-bean soup stand out in my memory.

It would have been so easy for us to never meet our condo neighbors. We mostly use our more private backdoor to enter and leave the condo, which means we wouldn't have run into them in the shared hallway. We could have let the *thunk* continue without inquiring as to what was causing it. Modern life has more ways to separate us than bring us together. Among adults under 30, 23% say that they don't know any of their neighbors, and 57% of Americans in general say they only know some of their neighbors (Davis and Parker 2019).

Building a village means participating in the village. By helping move a couch at 10 p.m. that random Sunday evening, my partner planted the seeds for our soup swap. The outreach to another couple was the movement that carried us into a friendship with them, and in doing so ended up saving us money on groceries and labor on cooking a few times. We had meals prepared for us by others without the exchange of money. We had resources freely given, without the expectation of being paid back.

When we think about wealth and wealth building, social wealth needs to be part of the conversation. And all too often, it isn't. The bootstraps narrative is embedded so deeply into the veins and hearts of Americans that sharing, collaboration, and investing in social capital is not only ignored, but it's actively looked down on. It is seen as embarrassing to ask for help feeding your kids. It is considered a burden on your friends to ask them to pick you up from the airport. You should be able to do all of this yourself, and if you can't, you're a failure.

Self-made is a mythology in the US that almost everyone believes in. Let us never forget when Kylie Jenner, born into one of the most famous families on the planet, was crowned a self-made billionaire by *Forbes*. It was the connections, money, and platforms that her family had that contributed to her ability to create and sell her makeup line. Jeff Bezos's parents gave him a cash loan of $245,573 for him to start Amazon in 1995. (Adjusted for inflation, that would be $501,686 in 2023 dollars.) Harper Lee was gifted a year of living expenses so that she could write the American classic *To Kill a Mockingbird* by her friends Michael and Joy Brown. Without their connections and communities, none of these people would be the successes they turned out to be.

No one is self-made. Your best work is never done alone. From financial loans, to donated time or labor, to emotional support, we all rely on one another for help as we achieve things. To really create these big-picture changes in our money and our world, we need each other. We can't borrow something if we have no one else in our community. We can't trade resources if there's no one else around. Community builds resilience in every sense of the word. Uncles pick up their nieces from soccer practices when their parents have to work late. A friend takes you to the airport at 8 a.m. on a Saturday morning. These actions save us money, strengthen our connection to others, and help us live complete lives.

Judd Manor is a senior living community in Cleveland, Ohio. Nestled in the University Circle area, it's closely located to museums, restaurants, and outdoor spaces. Living at Judd Manor comes with transportation service, yard maintenance, health care, and live music provided by the college students who live in the community for free.

In 2010, Judd Manor piloted a program with the Cleveland Institute of Music where one graduate student was granted free housing at the senior living center in exchange for once-a-month live performances at all three of Judd Manor's locations. Cleveland, like all major US cities, has experienced a housing crisis over the last two decades, and many colleges in the area have struggled to find enough affordable housing for their students. Judd Manor is an 18-minute walk from the Institute's campus and had the room to host a student.

The program was an "instant success," in the senior residents' own words. Residents reported feeling invigorated by the sight of a younger person in their day-to-day lives, and the live musical performances inspired some residents to get back into playing music themselves. By 2015, a total of five students lived for free at Judd Manor, and the program had extended to students at the Cleveland Institute of Art and, in 2016, to students at Case Western University.

There is the formal agreement, where the students perform monthly, but both the students and the senior residents report that the intergenerational living has been a net positive for their social and mental health. Both seniors and students report a familial-like bond that has developed, where they share meals, conversations, and even household tasks such as dog walking with one another. A group of ongoing studies from the National Institute on Aging shows that "positive indicators of social well-being may be associated with lower levels of interleukin-6. . . an inflammatory factor implicated in age-related disorders such as Alzheimer's disease, osteoporosis, rheumatoid arthritis, cardiovascular disease, and some forms of cancer" (National Institute on Aging 2020).

Inviting college students to live in a senior home may not seem like an obvious connection, but for most of human history people have lived in intergenerational homes. Taking into account the challenges of building more housing in an already developed area, the idea of simply opening up existing housing in the area to a new type of person makes the most sense. The old saying "If you want to go fast, go alone. If you want to go far, go together" is the perfect descriptor of how we need to approach things in a climate-stable future.

ACTIVITIES:

Outline three challenges in your life today. What are the things stressing you out the most in life or in your money? What have you been struggling with for more than six months and still haven't found a solution for? What do you wish you could change about your life?

_____

_____

_____

_____

What kind of solution feels good to you? Is it something that you *do* (such as joining an exercise group to help meet your fitness and friend goals)? Or is it something you *have* (such as a place where you can work on your novel without the kids interrupting you)? Identify the way you'd like the solution to your challenge to show up in your life.

_____

_____

_____

_____

Now, the *how*! Brainstorm three ways you can achieve this solution without needing to spend money. (Can you offer to work the front desk of a co-working space in exchange for 10 hours of free time a week to work there? Can you join a pick-up soccer league?)

_____

_____

_____

_____

Okay, here comes the accountability to continue your efforts! Right now, look at your calendar and find the time for you to do this thing, or work toward your solution. Speak to other people in your life about this if needed, such as parents or a partner. Mark the time off in your calendar for at least a month. Four straight weeks of working on something is long enough to make some progress, or to see how it's not working for you.

CHAPTER SIX

SUSTAINABLE INVESTING AND HOW TO BEAT FINANCIAL EMOTIONAL OVERLOAD

Only when the last tree has been cut down, the last fish been caught, and the last stream poisoned, will we realize we cannot eat money.

—Native American proverb, first recorded in 1972
and attributed to Alanis Obomsawin

I played lacrosse in college, and each spring break we traveled from cold and wet Connecticut to bright and warm Florida for a week of sprints and scrimmages in the sunshine. It certainly wasn't the spring break seen in the movies, but my team played many games of Uno, took trips to the movie theater, and cooked together throughout the week.

We also drank Gatorade and bottled water like it was going out of business. Plus, we had to grocery shop for the week for ourselves, which meant containers of deli meat, cans of sparkling water, and cartons upon cartons of eggs. And each year, we spread across three or four condos that didn't have a recycling center. All of our Gatorade bottles would be tossed into the trash, doomed to sit in a Florida landfill for the next 500 years, until they eventually break down into microplastics and make their way to the ocean, where some poor manatee would ingest them.

Not on my watch. One thing about me: when I get into something, I get *into* something. I put various teammates in charge of managing their plastic bottle situation in their condo and bringing them all to me at the end of the week. Before we hopped on our flights back to Connecticut, I would wrangle my assistant coach into driving me and the piles of plastic bottles to the nearest recycling center. One year it was a 40-minute drive each way; my coach definitely thought I was crazy.

I simply couldn't abide the idea of all our plastic bottles going into the trash when I knew that about 23 million tons of plastic wind up in water systems around the world every single year (UN Environmental Programme 2024). Beaches and rivers and lakes around the world have Gatorade and Dasani bottles bobbing along them as you're reading this, which are slowly leaching into the water itself and coming back to bite us and our animal friends in the butt in the form of microplastics.

After I graduated, I continued to be mildly obsessed with recycling and trying to get my trash to the right spot so as to minimize its impact on the Earth. I stopped using those flimsy plastic bags they offer in the produce section of the grocery store and made my own produce bags out of an old pillowcase. I carried my groceries home in reusable tote bags I had gotten for free at conferences and professional events. I'm the proud owner of one reusable water bottle that I've had since 2018.

And then I found out that only about 9% of all plastic, since the creation of plastic, has even successfully been recycled. This piece of information hit me like a Mack truck going 100 miles an hour. I had spent hours of my life devoted to recycling since I was a kid. I had petitioned apartment buildings I lived in to add a recycling bin next to the trash dumpster, and I had even carried my own cans and bottles out of events to recycle at home. *And it had all been for basically nothing?*

It honestly felt like "why bother?" The system is so large, the companies out there are making so many plastic bottles each year (with Coca-Cola admitting it made 200,000 plastic bottles *per minute* in 2017 alone), what was the point of my efforts? (Laville 2019). What could I do in the face of these corporations that were much bigger, much richer, and much more powerful than I was? I hung my head and for a few months admitted defeat.

It wasn't until a friend mentioned the subreddit, r/fucknestle, in a conversation about which companies we hated the most that something clicked in my brain. This subreddit was full of people who genuinely, deeply, hated Nestle and its corporate practices. (Which include stealing water from public communities and indigenous communities and using child labor to harvest cocoa used in their chocolate bars.) Their hatred ran so deep they needed a place to talk about it with other people in the world, and in that subreddit they traded tips to avoid buying Nestle products, ways that people could write to Nestle to advocate for changing corporate policies, and alternative products that were less of an ethical trainwreck.

A light bulb went off in my head. Instead of simply trying to sort out the aftermath of bad company policies and spending half my life trying to get one plastic water bottle recycled, I could use my money to force companies to change from the top down. I could withhold money from companies that I disagreed with and put my money toward companies I thought were doing the right thing. I could use money as a tool in the world in an active way. I wasn't just a bystander; I was a financial revolutionary.

INVESTING WHEN YOU'RE A HATER

When I talk to people about ethical investing, I get met with looks of skepticism. "Don't you know there's no ethical consumption under capitalism? Don't you know these companies control our lives and we have no power?" they say to me. "It's better to focus on just yourself. Go enjoy your life."

Hating the system feels good. Hating clears your skin and waters your crops! I have no problem with pointing out the many flaws in our world and our money systems. But I do have a problem with apathy. Tapping out because the work may be hard is not a choice in my mind, because the stakes are literally life and death. We hold so much power in our collective hands that when we all opt in, we can make drastic changes.

That's what sustainable investing offers us. A realistic way of looking at our problematic world and saying, "Here is a way we can make an impact while also making sure that we ourselves are taken care of." Instead, we're going to invest our money in the companies that make sense for all of our futures.

WHERE TO START: BUILDING YOUR GREEN MONEY PLAN

I like to think about my green money plan as a house. My foundation is my cash savings, stored at a green bank. My first floor is my retirement investment accounts, put into green investments. My second floor is my community building and mutual aid, helping me build social capital. And my attic is diversifying my investments into other areas outside the stock market.

This is what we'll build for you in this chapter!

WHAT ARE YOU SAVING AND INVESTING FOR?

Most people invest for the future. But what does that future look like, for you and the planet? What are you investing for?

This might be the first time someone has asked you to think in detail about what you want your long-term future to look like, and you might be drawing a blank. That's okay! It just means it's time to let your imagination run wild. What do you want to do with your one wild and precious life (to paraphrase Mary Oliver)? Once we know that, we can plug numbers into the dream to figure out what kind of investing plan you need to make it a reality.

Determine Your Retirement Number: The Rule of 25 or 30

How much money do you need to have invested to be able to retire? In the money nerd world, we like to say that retirement is a number, not an age. If you have enough money to retire at 30, you *can* retire at 30. You don't have to wait until 65. (It's okay if you don't have that kind of money at 30—I didn't! And at 35 I still don't!)

Figuring out how much money we will need thirty, forty years in the future is a little bit tricky. Luckily, there is a simple formula we can start with to get an idea of our retirement number, and then we can fine-tune from there.

"The rule of 25" is what we call the formula. It says to take your estimated annual retirement spending and multiply it by 25. This gives you the number you need to hit to be able to live in retirement for 25 years. As an example, if you want to spend $50,000 a year in retirement, you will take $50,000 and multiply it by 25. That gives you $1,250,000 as the amount you need to have before you can retire.

For longer retirements, you would increase your number. For example, if you want to retire at 30 and assume you will live until 90, your rule would be a rule of 60. We'll start with rule of 25 as a baseline, since most Americans retire in their 60s. As you clarify what you want retirement and perhaps financial freedom to look like for yourself, you can play around with your numbers.

But how did we determine we need $50,000 a year in retirement in the first place? We do a little math, a little dreaming, and a little research!

1. Choose where you'll live in retirement. Do you plan to stay where you are or do you want to move somewhere else? What are the housing costs in your chosen retirement location? What are food costs? Do some research on the major lifestyle costs in your chosen retirement location.

2. Consider what you want to *do* in retirement. Are you planning to hang out on the beach all day? Do you want to be traveling with your partner for six months of the year? Will you spend your days creating the most epic garden of all time? Design your lifestyle and do some research into current costs. Add 3%–5% inflation, and you'll have a good idea of what your retirement lifestyle will cost in a few decades.

3. Check your Social Security/pension benefits. You can do this by visiting ssa.gov or by checking your pension website. Roughly how much money do you think you'll get from each source when you are 65?

Now we have an idea of what you'll need. And it's okay if this number changes! It probably will as you get closer to making it a reality. You might not have the same vision for life at 25 that you do at 45. Remember that money is creative, so feel free to get creative with your financial planning.

Let's use $1,250,000 for our retirement number. It's big and maybe a little scary to look at, but you've got time and a lot of creativity on your side. With this number we can start building your financial house, and the first step is to figure out an ethical place to keep your money.

The foundation of your sustainable financial house is where you keep your checking and savings accounts, i.e. where you bank. The first floor is your spending plan, or your budget. The second floor is your brokerage, or where you do your investing and which companies you invest in. And your attic? That's the causes and people where you choose to spend your personal time and energy.

So let's build your financial house together! Start with the foundation: your bank.

Whom you bank with matters! Spoiler alert: the big national banks are not the place to make sustainable money moves from. Banks such as Chase, Bank of America, Wells Fargo, and CitiBank are the four biggest fossil fuel funders in the US. In the seven years after the 2015 Paris Climate Agreement, Chase Bank alone poured $434.15 billion into fossil fuel projects such as drilling for oil in the Arctic or fracking projects. What does that mean? It means they take their money (which is in part *your* money, if you use them as a bank) and invest it in projects such as drilling in the Arctic, fracking in Texas, or gas pipelines through Indigenous lands.

Fossil fuels, as we've already discussed, are the number-one thing contributing to climate change. So banks using their money to snatch more fossil fuels out of the ground and turn them into greenhouse gases is a huge problem and one you might not want your money to be a part of.

THE AREAS OF YOUR MONEY YOU CAN CONTROL

When it comes to making your money greener and more sustainable, there are three areas of your money that you have control over:

1. the banks you choose to keep your money in

2. the brokerage you choose to do your investing at
3. the investments you choose

Think of it kind of the way you approach grocery shopping. You don't set the price of bread at the grocery store, but you can choose which brand of bread you buy. For creating a sustainable money plan, where you keep your money matters a lot. It's the primary way to use your money as a tool to build a better world.

A QUICK EXPLANATION OF HOW BANKS WORK

Banks are two things at the same time: a place for people to store money long- and short-term, and companies themselves, looking to make a profit. Banks play a crucial role in the overall economy by acting as the intermediate between savers and borrowers. When you, a bank customer, deposit money into a bank, you're essentially entrusting the bank with your money.

The bank then uses that money for various purposes, including investments. We call the process by which banks utilize customers' money for investments "fractional reserve banking."

Fractional reserve banking is a fancy way of saying that banks are required to hold only a *fraction* of their customers' deposits as reserves. The rest of the deposited funds can be lent out or invested. So if 100 customers put in $1 million, the bank needs to keep only a portion of that $1 million *in* the bank—the rest they can invest in things to make money. This system allows banks to leverage their available capital, generating income through interest on loans and investments. The reserves are held to meet withdrawal demands and maintain the stability of the financial system.

One primary way banks use customers' money for investments is through lending. Banks provide loans to individuals, businesses, and governments, earning interest on the money they lend. Mortgages, personal loans, and business loans are common examples of how banks deploy customer deposits to make themselves money. The interest charged on these loans constitutes a major source of revenue for banks.

A 2022 report from Banking on Climate Chaos (2024) shows that US banks dominate fossil fuel financing, accounting for 28% of all fossil fuel financing in 2022. That means these banks partially use your money to open new coalmines or drill into the ocean floor looking for oil.

It's a climate disaster, but it's not one your money has to be part of.

CHOOSING A GREEN BANK

Albert Carter is a soft-spoken programmer from Alabama. He considers himself a long standing environmentalist, stemming from his experiences as a child along the Alabama Bayou.

"My mom is Vietnamese, and a lot of the Vietnamese community, people who are transplanted from the Vietnam War, just moved to the bayou and became shrimpers. My mom worked as a translator, as an interpreter for the community. And when Deepwater happened, and that oil rig blew up, I got, like, a very intimate view into what was happening there, which was very upsetting to me. Suddenly their [the shrimpers'] livelihood was devastated. And it was just some incredibly nasty, terrible stuff that happened to those people because of BP, with its continuing actions," Albert remembers.

Deepwater Horizon was an offshore deep-sea oil drilling rig. Basically it was a big boat, with equipment designed to drill into the seafloor and bring oil to the surface. In April 2010, the drilling from the rig caused a methane explosion, which grew into a fireball visible from 40 miles away. The drilling ship caught fire, killing 11 crewmen and injuring 17 more. The mix of oil and methane created a fire that was inextinguishable, despite being literally surrounded by water. The fire burned for 48 hours, spewing more methane into the atmosphere before the ship finally sank. The underwater oil well at the seabed continued to leak oil the entire time, and for years afterward. At least 134 million gallons of oil leaked into the Gulf of Mexico, poisoning fish populations, and killing an unknown number of marine animals. (We can estimate in the multimillions.) Deepwater remains one of the most ecologically devastating events in corporate American history.

Albert's experience with the repercussions of environmental disaster stuck with him as he built out his software engineering career. When he was furloughed in 2020 due to Covid, he wanted a way to fill his time. He ended up writing a blog post for Extinction Rebellion, a non-partisan movement that uses direct action to "persuade governments to act justly on the Climate and Ecological Emergency." His blog post focused on the climate impact of banks—where the money you put into a bank went, how banks funded climate change, and the truth of what banks do with money generally.

"When you do software, you can, you know, make things bigger, you can automate things, you can create a force multiplier," says Albert.

For people interested in environmental causes, the advice given to help slow climate change is often based in lifestyle choices: Eat less meat. Stop using plastic. No more straws. But to Albert, the connection between banks and climate change was already well established. What was needed was a force multiplier—something that could give the environmental movement more power to make large-scale changes faster.

"And so, the next multiplier to me seemed to be finance. Most fossil fuel finance is debt based, simply because the interest rates are lower. So just the same way a bank gives you a loan for your house, you know, gives you a mortgage, they can do the same thing for an oil rig, or a tanker or whatever it is. And the reason for that is that the interest rates [for these projects] are lower. And if the company doesn't pay back the loan, then the bank can repossess whatever it is that's there for collateral," Albert explains.

To Albert, this lending was the most logical thing to concentrate climate efforts on. If people stopped using the banks that funded major fossil fuel projects around the globe, there would be less funding for these projects, and this would have the biggest impact on slowing climate change.

Force, meet multiplier.

Bank Green is the project that grew out of that blog post. A completely volunteer-run project, Bank Green's mission is to help people stop funding fossil fuels through where they bank. The homepage has a bar where you can search your bank name to see whether they are investing in oil, gas, or coal.

Thanks to tools such as Bank Green, you as an individual have more options to find a green bank and to divest from the banks polluting our world. Here's how to choose a green bank today:

- Avoid the big four: Chase, Bank of America, Citi Bank, and Wells Fargo. Using almost any other bank than these four is a much greener choice than any of them, due to the amount of fossil fuel funding they do.
- Use a tool such as Bank Green to research whether your current bank invests in fossil fuels.
- Use a tool such as Mighty Deposits to check whether your credit union invests in fossil fuels.

SUSTAINABLE INVESTING 101

Now that we have the foundation of your green money home, let's talk about investing. For this, I want to start at the very beginning: What even is investing? How does the stock market work?

Investing is the idea of taking some of your paycheck and putting it into another business so that that business can expand and, ideally, become more valuable. The piece of the company that you buy is called a stock, or sometimes called a share.

When a company decides it wants to join the stock market and sell these shares to people like you and me, it does something called an initial public offering, or IPO for short. (You may remember that Roblox had an IPO in 2021, and Airbnb had an IPO in 2020.) During an IPO the company sets a fixed amount of shares to sell, sometimes to just high-level investors (such as investment banks with billions of dollars) or to the general public. Whoever buys that stock now owns a direct piece of that company. Once the company enters a stock exchange (think of a stock exchange as the place you go to buy shares, like a storefront), other investors and businesses can buy it, and the IPO ends. Essentially, an IPO is a company's debut, where they go from being totally privately owned (like my company is privately owned by me!) to opening themselves up to other investors.

Once a company is in the stock market, if you buy $5,000 in shares of a company, you are buying from another shareholder. If a company has big news, for instance, Apple announcing a new iPad, more people may buy the stock, causing the value of the stock to go up. For you as the investor, your share becomes more valuable than it was when you bought it. That means you also can make a profit, if you decide to sell your share at the higher price and pocket the difference. (After paying taxes of course. Uncle Sam never forgets.)

If Apple launches a product that does poorly, the value of Apple stock goes down. This is common; the value of companies ebbs and flows with things such as the state of the world, the state of the economy, and the state of that specific company. If Apple lays off half its workforce worldwide and decides to stop making MacBooks, it's a pretty good bet the value of Apple stock will go down. As an owner of Apple, that means your investment portfolio would also be pulled down.

This is the risk inherent with any investment, and it's why it's crucial to diversify your investments, whether that's in the stock market or anywhere else.

Don't put all your money into a single company or industry (e.g. don't just buy tech companies, and don't just buy one tech company). Instead put your money into multiple companies, across multiple sectors. A strong portfolio is one that has balances built into it; as an example, you've invested in Apple, Target, and Disney. These are three different companies, in different sectors of service, that offer different things to their customers. If Disney goes bankrupt, you wouldn't lose everything you've got because you have two other totally separate companies in your investment portfolio.

Investing in the stock market is something every wealthy person in the United States does. When we say that Bill Gates is worth $125 billion, he's not keeping that under his mattress or in a savings account. The vast bulk of that is the value of the shares of Microsoft that he owns.

But what if you don't want to support Apple? Or Exxon Mobil? Or Tesla? Is the world of investing still open to you? Are you destined to die penniless in an open field somewhere, watching while the CEO of Shell pours oil directly into a baby duckling's mouth?

Actually, no. While our system has many and varied flaws, there are also options to use your money as a tool and redirect where you put your dollars and what you support with your dollars.

Sustainable investing is one such option. **Now, I want to be clear:** there is no one single investment that will be perfectly ethical to everyone on the planet and that only goes up and never loses any money. Ethical investing, or sustainable investing, should really be called "I'm doing my best in a complicated world" investing. *Please release the expectation for yourself or others of being the perfect investor, the same way we released expectations of being a perfect consumer.*

Here's some investing lingo you need to know before we dive into crafting your sustainable investing plan.

Investing account: This is the place where you invest your money. A 401(k), an IRA, a 403(b), a SEP IRA—these are all investing accounts. Think of an account like a boat. A boat is designed to transport items. The boat itself houses the items on its journey. Your 401(k) houses your actual investments; it's not an investment itself.

Assets: This is a fancy money word for "things that can make you money." Stocks, bonds, and real estate can all be considered financial assets. In the stock market world, we consider things such as stocks, bonds, and cash as investable assets.

Asset allocation: This means "how you divide and organize the things that make you money," aka how much money you invest in stocks versus how much you keep in cash versus how much you invest in bonds. It's a pie chart of where you keep your money. You don't want to go all in just one company or one type of asset. That's very risky because that one thing could go bankrupt and leave you with nothing. Diversification is important for a strong stock market portfolio!

Stocks: Stocks, aka shares, are pieces of publicly traded companies that you buy via the stock market. Stocks are a representation of ownership in a company. Stocks are sold by companies to raise money to grow the business. If you've ever heard someone say, "I own 500 shares of Google," that means they bought 500 teeny-tiny pieces of ownership in Google. Now the performance of these 500 shares is tied to the performance of Google. You buy a stock and you put it in your account, so you would keep your 500 shares of Google in your 401(k), for example.

Bonds: Bonds are another type of investment you can buy, but they work more like loans than like stocks do. When you buy a bond, you're giving the company who issued it a loan, and the company agrees to pay you back the value of the loan on a specific date and pay you interest along the way. Think about student loans: you borrowed $10,000 to go to Harvard and agreed to pay back your lender at 5% interest over 10 years. That's how bonds work, except you are the one getting the money in this case!

Interest: Interest in the investing world is money your money earns. In the stock market, if you buy a share of Apple for $10,000 and then Apple ends the year having grown 5%, you would now have $10,500. If you buy another $10,000 the next year, you are now earning future interest off $20,500, even though you only contributed $20,000. The average stock market return, adjusted for inflation, has been 7% a year.

Brokerage: A brokerage firm is a company that connects buyers and sellers to the stock market. Through a brokerage, investors buy, sell, and trade stocks, bonds, and things such as index funds. Common brokerages in the US are Vanguard, Fidelity, and Charles Schwab. Brokerages charge fees to buy and sell via their platforms.

Fund: Index, mutual, or exchange-traded funds (ETFs) are bundles of companies. They get grouped together based on the fact that they have something in common. Maybe it's the type of company they are (e.g. a health-care fund would have only health-care companies in it) or the current valuation of the company (trillion-dollar companies get grouped together). Think of a fund like a bouquet of flowers. You can get a bouquet of 12 roses, but they are all roses. Or you can get a bouquet that has roses, lilies, and carnations in it. They are all flowers, but different flowers. By buying the one bouquet, you pay one price for three different flowers.

Expense ratio: This is an annual fee you will pay for owning a fund. This fee goes to the people or company who manages the fund; it's an admin fee. It is always a percentage, such as 0.08% or 1%. The percentage is applied to the total you have invested in the fund. So if you have an expense ratio of 0.08% and you have $10,000 invested, you will pay $8 total. Ideally you want to find funds with a low expense ratio.

Sector: The area that a company is in. BlueCross BlueShield, for example, is a health insurance company in the US. Therefore, it's in the health-care sector. Google would be in the technology sector. You can review the different sectors that are included in a fund by reviewing the fund's "prospectus," which is a fancy way of saying a fund's 101 explainer. (Learning the sector is a huge part of sustainable investing!)

BDS: An acronym that stands for boycott, divest, sanctions. This is a type of political and social action that's been used to create change on various social and financial causes for hundreds of years.

ESG: An acronym that stands for environmental, social, governance. If a fund or individual company has an ESG rating or notification, they have some sort of mandate or practice where they consider the environmental, social, and governance of the companies within the fund as part of their financial analysis and business approach. For example, an index fund that abstains from including fossil fuel companies would get a high ESG rating.

Your first starting point for understanding ethical investing is the acronym *ESG*. It's kind of like the organic label that gets put on food; it lets you know that this company, or this fund, is making an attempt to do the right thing.

SUSTAINABLE INVESTING STRATEGIES FOR YOUR IRA

Now that we understand how investing works, how do we do it? Where do we start? I always recommend that you start with retirement accounts. The best-case scenario for all of us is that we will get old! And old us is going to need money for food, housing, and comfortable caftans!

Firstly, what are the values you're looking to express financially? Many things are important to us all: racial justice, gender equality, prison abolition, environmental protections. But in our complicated world, there is no one company that is perfect on *all* these topics and others. To begin your sustainable investing journey, I want you to pick *two* values: one you want to actively avoid with your money and one you want to actively fund with your money.

For me, that was clean energy and fossil fuels. I want my money to actively fund clean energy companies, and I want to actively avoid fossil fuels in my investments. For other things I feel passionate about, such as affordable housing, I volunteer my time with local organizations looking to expand the building of affordable housing units and reclaiming empty buildings to be used for housing.

None of us can or should hold our money to a standard of perfection. If I waited to invest to fund a company that was perfect on gender roles, racial justice, and the environment, I would never invest. I can accept that a company might not have any women in positions of leadership *if* they have a strong environmental initiative for my investments. We need to hold duality for ourselves and our investments in our imperfect world!

At the end of this chapter we have some exercises for you to help you determine your sustainable investing values.

Investments go inside investment accounts. Things such as a 401(k), 403(b), or a Roth IRA, these are all investment accounts. Opening one does not make you an investor. There's a difference between an investment account and an investment. Think of it this way: when you go to the clothing store and walk around, you are shopping. But unless you buy a shirt, going to the store alone doesn't mean you have new clothes. Same thing with investing. You can open an investing account, such as a 401(k), but if you don't put anything in it, for example, Apple stock, you don't own any investments.

Now, on to which investment account you should start with. I consider the IRA to be the most democratic investing account available in the US because they are not tied to workplaces and anyone who is 18+ with earned income can open one. IRA stands for individual retirement account. It's an investing account where current you can stash cash for future you!

An account like a 401(k) is significantly less accessible, since only people in privately owned companies have access to one. A self-employed person, or public school teacher, would not be able to use a 401(k), but both could use an IRA.

(PS, something else important about an IRA is that you do not have to be a full US citizen to open one! If you are a legal resident, you can open an IRA and invest in the stock market!)

There are two main types of IRAs: Roth and traditional. The Roth is infinitely more popular, and you may have seen TikTok videos about them or heard a friend talk about them.

Here's Your Roth IRA 101

A Roth IRA is an individual retirement account that allows you to invest after-tax dollars and then provides tax-free growth and withdrawals in retirement. Taxwise, you pay the taxes when you contribute the money, and then, once you're 59½ or older and you've had the account open for at least five years, you can withdraw money without paying federal taxes.

Via your Roth IRA, you can invest in individual stocks, individual bonds, ETFs, index funds, and mutual funds. The maximum amount of money you can put into a Roth IRA in 2024 is $7,000.

The government does keep its eye on who gets to contribute to Roth IRAs. In 2024, the single tax filers earning over $161,000 MAGI (modified adjusted gross income) can't open a Roth IRA. The government thinks you make too much money to utilize one. If married and filing jointly, your joint MAGI must be under $240,000. These income limits *and* contribution limits change every few years, so if you're reading this in 2026 or beyond, take to the Internet to check the new limits.

(If you make more than the income limits for a Roth IRA, you should open a traditional IRA! It's got different perks but still is more democratic than the workplace retirement plans.)

The Roth IRA also comes with some very chic perks such as:

The ability to withdraw your contributions tax free after having the account for five years. Because you've already paid taxes on the money, the government allows you to withdraw your contributions if you want. Ideally you will *not* do this, because the whole point of investing is to give the money decades to grow, but it is a worst-case scenario emergency fund. You *cannot* withdraw the earnings if you're under 59½, unless you become disabled, without paying an early withdrawal penalty.

The ability to withdraw up to $10,000 over your lifetime specifically for a first-time downpayment. This can be very helpful for first-time home buyers!

To open an IRA, you need to pick a brokerage. There are brokerages such as Carbon Collective that have a specific mission to divest from fossil fuels in order to create industry change. You can also use a larger company such as Vanguard and then simply opt into more specific sustainable companies or funds.

I recommend that you don't get too hung up on which brokerage you pick. While some are definitely more sustainable than others, when it comes to a sustainable investing strategy, which investments you buy is much more important that where you do the investing. Not all of us have access to a sustainable brokerage, especially if you are investing through a workplace retirement plan.

SUSTAINABLE INVESTING STRATEGIES TO MAKE YOUR MONEY GREENER

When it comes to deciding what you want in your ethical portfolio, there are three main sustainable investing strategies you can implement to keep the garbage companies out and the better companies in.

Negative screening: You can use negative screening to eliminate certain companies or types of sectors that do not align with your values from your investment search. The process of screening in general is like searching for clothes in an online store; you can filter the clothes according to size, color, or type. Negative screening allows you to do the same thing with your investments. You can filter *out*, for example, companies that make guns or fossil fuel companies.

Positive screening: The flipside of negative screening, positive screening allows you to filter only for companies that *do* align with your values. With positive screening you'll be matched with companies that are in sectors you want to support or have missions that you agree with.

Impact investing: This is a strategy where you support funds or individual companies that are focused on creating a specific change in the world. Investing in a clean energy fund that aims to build 400 new solar power plants per year to help transition off fossil fuels would be an example of impact investing.

Divesting: Divesting is when you get rid of your investments that do not align with your values. Many of us, when we start investing, pick an index fund or mutual fund that someone else tells us is "good." I find in my one-on-one work most people have no idea what they're investing in. Divesting is the process of saying, "Oh, I have $10,000 invested into Chevron. I will get rid of that because I hate Chevron."

You can use one or all of these strategies in your investment portfolio. I used negative screening to filter out fossil fuels and impact investing to find companies focused on building solar energy panels when I was putting together my investment strategy.

Where do you do the research with these strategies? You can type "ESG funds + your brokerage" into Google, and it's likely you'll be taken to a page where Vanguard or Schwab, or whatever your brokerage is, shares their more sustainable fund options.

From there, click the ticker symbol (the combination of letters next to the longer fund name. For example, Amazon's ticker symbol is AMZN), and you'll get taken to a page with more information on that specific fund. Now is where you can root around and get the details on what companies are in this fund and decide whether you like them or not!

Click on "Holdings" or "Portfolio Makeup"—you're looking for wording that tells you what's in the fund. Once there, you'll be shown information on the sectors covered by this fund, as well as the top 10 holdings in the fund. Those are the 10 biggest and most valuable companies in the fund. Take a look at them; how do you feel about them? Are you seeing any stinkers? Feeling good about what you see?

If you want to see *all* the companies in the fund, you'll look for the word "Prospectus" and click on that. This usually opens a PDF that has several pages of information on the fund, including the fees, past performance, who manages the fund, and most importantly, all the companies in the fund. Here you can go through one by one if you want to see everything you're investing in.

This is the nitty-gritty way to really make sure your money is as sustainable or ethical as possible. It takes a little bit of time, but you can find investments within an hour usually. *If you'd like to make the time even shorter, we have some more search tools listed at the end of this chapter.*

PUTTING IT ALL TOGETHER
The 6 Investments Strategy

Let's get back to building our green money house!

Our foundation is choosing a green bank—we covered that.
Our first floor is retirement investing—that's going to be our IRA.
Our second floor is community building—that's in Chapter 5.
Our attic is diversifying—let's talk about that!

Once your IRA is open and you have chosen your sustainable investing strategy, you'll do research on specific investments you want to buy. Generally I tell people that you only need one to three sustainable funds, and one to three sustainable individual companies for the entirety of your portfolio. If that sounds too simple, breathe a sigh of relief: the people trying to make you think investing is hard are the ones who make money off you thinking that! Investing can be super-simple, and sustainable investing is no exception.

Why only six investments total? Don't you need more to protect yourself and actually grow your money? No, not really!

With the six-investment portfolio, I want you to invest in three funds and three individual companies. Remember that funds have many companies inside of them; you're buying one bouquet of flowers, but there are many different flowers in the bouquet. That means if you have three sustainable funds, and each fund has 300 companies inside it, you have invested in 900 companies. That's a very diversified portfolio already! You may own wind energy, health-care companies, publishers, and media companies, all within these funds.

The three individual companies you invest in are to tailor your portfolio to your personal ethics. You may select three women-owned companies, or three companies that focus on regenerative agriculture. When you purchase these companies, you are *only* purchasing these companies. They are not diversified. You might want a solar panel company, a company that cleans up old oil rigs, and a company that builds wells in developing countries. These are all different areas of business and sustainability, so you are diversified.

Creating a Six-Investment Portfolio

Here's an example of a six-investment portfolio. For this example, we'll say the companies we want to actively *avoid* are guns or weapons manufacturers, and the value we want to actively *support* is gender equity.

Knowing that, we will use negative screening to exclude companies that produce weapons from our search. You can do this in two easy ways: head to your brokerage website (so Fidelity.com, Vanguard.com, Robinhood .com) and search "ESG funds" in the search bar. This will bring you to the information and funds your brokerage has that fall broadly under ESG investing. There's also a website called As You Sow that has a specific gun-free funds list you can look through!

From this first round of search, you should be presented with a list of funds available that do not include gun producers. Your next step is to find the ticker symbol and look at the prospectus to see which companies are included.

One gun-free fund I found has the ticker symbol AMINX. When I look at the top 10 holdings they include companies such as Microsoft, Eli Lilly and Co., and Genuine Parts Co. No Smith & Wesson here! No Lockheed Martin here! Repeat this process for the other two funds you'd like to invest in.

Next, think about the three individual companies you'd like to support. In this example, we're looking at companies that support gender equity. You might start by finding companies that have a female CEO. As of this publication, Walgreens has a female CEO. Walgreens is a health-care and retail company, so for diversification, your second choice for an individual company may be something in hospitality.

Once you've selected the funds and companies, your main goal is to get as much money in them as possible! With this six-holding portfolio, your focus becomes trying to get money into the holdings so that they can grow. The earlier you invest, the more time your money has to compound, aka, the more time your money has to earn more money and help you reach your retirement number. That's why you see financial pros and money nerds say things such as "invest early!"

(Remember, funds usually have hundreds of companies in them, so when you buy a share of the fund, you are buying tiny pieces of all the companies in the fund. That's a way that you diversify your money.)

Don't worry about constantly checking the market or constantly looking for new companies. Keep your energy toward building up your holdings, and let compound interest work for you.

Investment Considerations

Once you find companies and funds you want to invest in that align with your values, there are some money considerations to take into account.

With traditional investing, the costs are the number-one consideration. The expense ratio and other fees such as transaction fees or a 401(k) fee are things to look out for. The more you pay in fees, the lower your profits will be. The higher the fees, the lower your profits will be.

With regard to sustainable investing, some sustainable funds are more expensive than unsustainable funds. Think of it this way; you can get an $8 shirt at Target. That shirt is cheap because it was made with cheap materials by someone likely in Bangladesh being underpaid. Or you can buy an ethically made shirt that costs $40 that was made with sustainable materials by someone paid a fair wage. The second shirt costs more because it was produced under better circumstances that cost more to maintain.

Some sustainable funds cost more because they include companies that are doing the right thing, and the right thing costs more money at the moment. Building new solar panels and getting them to people around the US costs money. More sustainable funds also exclude terrible companies that are profitable. Exxon Mobil is destroying the planet, but it's making a lot of money as it does so.

Consider costs when choosing your sustainable funds and individual companies. I also want you to consider:

- Diversification, aka buying in different sectors to spread your money out: Don't put all your eggs in one basket!

- Asset allocation: You also want to buy different types of investments, such as stocks and bonds *and* funds. These are all different investments, which means your money is further diversified.
- Investment risk: This generally refers to the type of investment you're buying and the expectation for profit from it. Are you buying the next Apple or the next Enron? Is this company already profitable? You can check past returns to see how the company did in previous years.
- Timeline to retirement: A 20-year-old can be more aggressive with their investments than a 60-year-old. How aggressive you are with your asset allocation should depend on how far you are from leaving full-time work.

OPTING OUT TOTALLY: LEAVING WALL STREET BEHIND

If you've read all this and simply cannot abide putting your money into any company that you are not 100% down with, you do have the option of completely opting out of the stock market. You do not have to invest in the stock market, or become a landlord, to build financial security for yourself.

In 2009, Laura Oldanie discovered the world of permaculture. Permaculture is an approach to agriculture design and production that mimics natural systems, with a focus on no waste and ecological diversity that strengthens the entire project from within. (Collecting rainwater in tanks to be used for showering and then repurposing the gray water from the shower tank to be filtered and used for irrigation to water plants would be an example of permaculture in action.)

Discovering permaculture awoke something inside Laura. If nature worked in a way where one thing was mutually beneficial for multiple projects, why didn't humans approach their finances this way? Living in St. Petersburg, Florida, Laura was living through a rapidly changing climate and dealing with the impact of stronger hurricanes year after year. To her, it made no sense to invest her money into the companies that created the problems she had to deal with on the front lines.

"In the midst of climate change it really feels like if I rely solely on [money], I'm going to leave myself in the lurch," Laura says. She decided to take her money out of stock investments as much as possible (she still has a small amount of money invested through an annuity that she cannot access or change due to the fee schedule) and redefine what financial security meant to her.

To Laura, it seemed that traditional financial advice and the general American lifestyle focused much too heavily on money itself. Money was part of life, of course, and Laura uses money in her life. But for her, life and security involved so much more than just numbers on a screen. Adopting the mindset of permaculture helped Laura determine that to her, financial security could be best determined through three things:

- community building
- local investments
- reducing her material needs

To accomplish that, Laura withdrew her money from the stock market and instead put it in smaller, local investments. She has invested in an organic farm in St. Petersburg, which pays her a small amount of interest in return for her investment. Laura met the owner of the farm through mutual friends, and had a discussion with them about permaculture and agriculture. This opened the door to a conversation about her investing in the farm, and the two mutually agreed upon the terms of investment. She owns her home outright, and has put in an additional dwelling unit (ADU), where she envisions a caretaker living for free one day when she is in need of assistance. To her, this is a symbiotic way to build financial security without needing the stock market. She will need help in her old age, and she can reciprocate that help by providing free housing.

Laura's financial stability doesn't rest on the rise of Wall Street, but it does depend heavily on the people around her and on her housing. Instead of relying on a 7% return from the stock market to meet her needs, she is relying on her community to meet her future needs. Today, she puts in considerable time with other people, doing things such as hosting dinner parties and going foraging together. This time investment is critical to her financial future the same way that investing money is critical to someone using the stock market's future.

Laura sums up her decision to leave Wall Street like this: "By putting so much emphasis on [money alone], I'm leading to the destruction of my future that I'm trying to prepare for." Turns out, for true financial freedom and security, "I need a lot more than money to feel secure." Community, housing security, and social capital is what Laura has spent the last decade of her life building. To her, these are the tangible things she needs to retire securely, rather than rely on putting her money into the financial performance of companies outside of her community.

ACTIVITIES:

What is your primary goal with more sustainable investing? To create a better world, to make money, to have your money somewhere that grows and allows you to sleep at night?

_____

_____

_____

_____

Determine your retirement number using the rule of 25 or 30.

_____

_____

Make a list of your values that you'd like to express financially (aka what are the areas you'd like to invest in? Green energy? Regenerative farming?

_____

_____

Make a list of companies or things you'd like to stay away from. (For me this is Nestle and companies that build private prisons.)

_____

_____

Talk to people about money and investments in your life—we're more likely to respond to people we know. If your parents know you have divested from private prisons, they are more likely to do the same!

COMPLETELY DIVEST

Here's how to take your money totally out of Wall Street and still build a healthy financial future.

Determine your retirement number and lifestyle. Where will you live? How much do you expect to need? Whom will you live with/near? Design your dream life!

_____

_____

_____

_____

Determine the rate of return you need from your investments to make a profit. For Laura, this was in the 2%–4% range.

_____

_____

List out the areas you would be interested in investing in (local agriculture, water projects, small businesses) and what connections you have to those communities.

_____

_____

_____

_____

Become active in communities in those areas that are looking for investors.

Draw up legal agreements for your investments/trades.

Resources

Third Act is an organization that helps people 60+ divest their retirement portfolios from environmentally harmful companies and helps them advocate at a legislative level for eco-friendly legislation.

My sustainable investing course—I have created the only sustainability-focused investing course on the market! (As of now.) The course focuses on stock market and real estate investing from an ethical, sustainable, and inclusive point of view. Find more info at www.karap.podia.com.

As You Sow is a fantastic nonprofit that helps track corporate actions in regard to pollution, environmental degradation, and climate action. They have a search tool where you can find out how your investments are ranked (from A to F) on sustainability.

CHAPTER SEVEN

GREENWASHING: WHAT TO LOOK FOR AND HOW TO AVOID IT

Right now, the planet cannot afford delays, excuses, or more greenwashing.

—Catherine Mckenna

"What happens here, stays here" is the famous (one might say infamous) slogan of America's playground, Las Vegas. Created in 2003, the slogan became iconic instantly, inspiring visitors to the city to live (and spend) as if they were creating legendary, even dangerous, memories for themselves. It's a marketing campaign that transcended simple sales to become a cultural call to action.

Anyone might be happy with that kind of success. But the same marketing firm arguably reached its highest acclaim in 2000 when it launched the "America's Power" campaign on behalf of Americans for Balanced Energy Choices (ABEC). The campaign centered on how important coal is as a fuel source for American life, powering everything from your television to the farm equipment that puts food on American tables. Coal, the ads said, was crucial to our lives and most importantly, it was *clean* energy. Clean coal, the ads claimed, was the way of the future.

Clean coal is one of the best greenwashing campaigns ever created. ABEC was created by some of the US's biggest fossil fuel companies: Peabody Energy (the biggest US coalmining corporation), Arch Coal (third-biggest US coalmining corporation), CONSOL Energy (fourth-biggest US coalmining corporation), and Foundation Coal (fifth-biggest US coalmining corporation) are all founding members.

Coal is one of the three big fossil fuels responsible for almost 90% of all carbon dioxide emissions globally. We mine coal from the ground and then burn it to create steam energy or send it through a combustion turbine to create electricity. When coal is burned, the carbon in the coal combines with oxygen to form carbon dioxide. Burning a pound of coal emits 2.07 pounds of carbon dioxide (EPA 2016).

The lie of clean coal was created because in the 1990s, coal was on the front lines of environmental activism. The Clean Air Act Amendments of 1990 strengthened rules to reduce production of acid rain and required states to produce a plan to reach national air quality standards. It also authorized states to put a moratorium on major polluters projects until the standards were reached. In 1997 the US signed the Kyoto Protocol, which committed signing countries to limit and reduce greenhouse gas pollution. Coalmines were closing in places such as West Virginia and Kentucky, and the conversation around green energy was growing. The Toyota Prius, the world's first mass-produced hybrid vehicle, had gone global in 2000. Toyota called it the "car for the 21st century" (Toyota Blog 2021).

Faced with the world truly awakening to how dangerous and damaging their product was, coal companies needed to take action. Coal was losing loyalty from its American audience, and most importantly, coal companies were losing money. Producing less coal would cut into their profit. Pivoting to clean energy would take time and billions in investment. Instead, they hired marketing firm R&R Partners to come up with the idea of clean coal. Why change when they could simply rebrand coal and keep doing exactly what they were doing?

Here's how clean coal was supposed to work: the negative effects of coal's carbon dioxide emissions would be captured before being released into the air and stored underground. This practice, called carbon capture and storage (CCS), was the center point of the advertising campaign. The campaign's mission was to convince the public that we didn't need to end coal usage; we just needed to add in CCS to make coal clean.

Unfortunately, clean coal was only a pipe dream. In order for CCS to work, new machinery would have to have been created and implemented in current coal refineries, and new coal refineries would have had to have been built. Both of these things would create new emissions. And the answer of putting the carbon dioxide underground was an incomplete one; carbon dioxide is a gas. We'd have to change the gas to a liquid and then try to store it underground at a temperature no higher than −78 degrees Celsius. This entire process is incredibly expensive, time consuming, and creates still more emissions, more than we'd be able to deduct from the process at all. It's kind of like if you approached saving money from the idea that you have to spend money on various places to keep your cash savings; a bucket, a bag, a locked box. Each item costs you money to acquire, therefore leaving you less and less to actually save.

YOU DON'T HAVE TO BE NICE TO THE BAD GUYS

Greenwashing is the practice of making false or misleading statements about the environment-friendly benefits or creation of a product or company. Clean coal is a particularly egregious example, but we see greenwashing in almost every industry today as the conversation about climate change has become mainstream.

Greenwashing bypasses the actual problem and puts a green Band-Aid on it. If fossil fuels are causing climate change, the solution to stopping climate change is to not use fossil fuels. Greenwashing is a marketing campaign from companies that want to continue business as usual, without their customers or advocates nagging at them about the root of the problem.

Spotting greenwashing is getting easier, mostly because companies are less able to hide in the shadows. With the growth of online review sites, and the understanding that not everything you see online can be trusted, consumers are more aware than ever before about where the items in their life come from. There are apps, such as Good on You, that rank companies' ethical behavior based on public information available from company websites, credible third-party reports, and certifications obtained. Secondhand stores and websites give people a chance to buy clothes at lower prices rather than support unethical companies.

Additionally, consumers seem to be more comfortable voicing their discontent with brands' behavior, particularly on social media. Social media has its downsides, but perhaps its most incredible strength is how it allows people from around the world to connect, share experiences, and fact-check people and companies in real time. One of the world's most popular companies recently experienced a social media smackdown due to their greenwashing.

In 2022, clothing company SHEIN became the most googled clothing brand on Earth (Haqqi 2022). It's a hugely impressive achievement for a brand founded in 2008, outranking heritage brands such as Chanel or globally popular Nike. SHEIN offers clothing at incredibly low price points, often offering dresses for $7 and tops for $5. They ship globally and have invested heavily in social media marketing, using influencers to reach their target audience of teenage girls and women in their 20s.

SHEIN's rise can largely be attributed to the pace at which they make clothing. According to an investigation by *Rest of World*, SHEIN added anywhere between 2,000 and 10,000 individual styles to its app each day between July and December of 2021. In *Inside the SHEIN Machine: UNTOLD*, a documentary from Channel 4, it was reported that workers receive a base salary of 4,000 yuan per month—roughly $556—to make 500 pieces of clothing per day. The clothing manufacturers' use of virgin polyester and of oil creates the same amount of CO_2 as approximately 180 coal-fired power plants (Synthetics Anonymous 2.0 2023).

SHEIN is a trendy environmental disaster.

Here's where social media connections enter the conversation. SHEIN has used TikTok heavily to promote their brand, sending influencers free clothes in exchange for creating try-on videos. This has made SHEIN a nearly constant topic of conversation on the app. In 2023, the conversation changed from #sheinhaul videos to #boycottshein videos on the app. SHEIN's unethical work practices and their terrible environmental impact had become mainstream enough to inspire pushback. Articles popped up in news outlets such as *Time magazine* and Reuters, and was covered extensively in the sustainable blog world. Individual creators on platforms such as TikTok and Instagram called for a buyer boycott.

An influencer trip completely backfired on the brand in June 2023. Influencer trips, for those not in the know, are where a brand flies a group of influencers out to a specific location and treats them to a vacation. In return the influencers make nonstop content promoting the brand for the entire trip and usually a period afterward. They are fantastic promotional tools, combining the draw that many non-influencers have to see behind the scenes of an influencer's life and the appetite online to see luxury accommodations, clothes, and experiences. SHEIN put together an influencer trip to regain control of their online narrative. The trip flew influencers to Guangzhou, China, to tour one of their production factories. They wanted the influencers' followers to see in real time that the company's operations were trustworthy and that their workers were treated well.

Online, there was almost instant backlash. Followers and commenters were furious, repeatedly calling out how this was a whitewashed trip, where the influencers were shown only one polished factory where the workers knew they would be on camera. The influencers were lambasted far and wide, and SHEIN came across as tone-deaf and sinister, trying to literally buy a good image.

The trip was a failed effort in greenwashing. Their greenwashing couldn't survive in the face of social media exposure and the bright light of investigative journalism. People could see their greenwashing a mile away, and they called SHEIN out for months over it.

In October 2023, after a summer of public relations disasters, SHEIN announced it would spend $7.6 million on a partnership with the nonprofit Apparel Impact Institute to create a plan for more energy-efficient production. The partnership will apply to more than 500 production facilities and SHEIN estimates the energy changes will result in 1.25 million fewer tons of greenhouse gas emissions each year. The company has also declared a goal of reducing supply chain emissions by 25% by 2030 and a focus on transitioning to renewable power for the company's manufacturing.

While SHEIN remains a major polluter, the online backlash created by everyday, normal customers, pushed the company to make internal changes. People used their voice to say, "Hey, your greenwashing isn't okay," and it resulted in tangible change. It's a lesson to us all that we don't need to be nice to the people that are ruining the planet for all of us.

HOW TO AVOID GREENWASHING WHEN YOU'RE JUST A REGULAR PERSON

Spotting greenwashing in your everyday spending will help you avoid companies lying to your face and make your money greener.

Look for Vague Promises or Pledges in Marketing Materials

Language such as "We use sustainable practices to create our products" can clue you into greenwashing. That sentence is incredibly vague; what does sustainable mean here? At what point in their supply chain are they being sustainable? What practices do they use, and what have they shifted away from?

Using "Sustainable" to Describe a Portion of Their Output

Many brands have a specific "sustainable" product or line. H&M, for example, has a line of clothing they claim is sustainable called "Conscious Collection," where they say they use 50% or more of recycled materials to make the clothes. But not all of their clothes are made this way. H&M produces more than 3 billion pieces of clothing per year, so even having a sustainable portion of their production doesn't offset the sheer size of unsustainable production.

Don't Let the Color Green Fool You

Many companies simply use *green*, or the image of a leaf or tree, in their marketing to subtly imply that they are a sustainable company. They're just betting that your brain will make a connection between the color green and the practice of sustainability! Check to see whether they have any sustainable practices or initiatives.

Words without Explanation Are Empty

Popular greenwashing phrases are terms such as "eco-friendly," "green," "earth-friendly," "non-toxic," "pure," and "raw." Without an explanation of what "raw" means to this brand and its creation process, these words are just greenwashing. Check their websites for more information on what their "non-toxic" ingredients are and where they come from.

Check for Certifications from Trusted Organizations

There are many organizations doing the legwork to make sure that brands are really walking the walk. Look for certifications from these organizations to be able to trust your purchase.

US Department of Agriculture (USDA) organic certification: The USDA certification requires meeting the S governments regulations around how a product is made from growth to manufacturing and must undergo an in-person, on site inspection.

Green Seal: Green Seal is a nonprofit that develops environmentally friendly standards for companies to comply with. Founded in 1989, Green

Seal tests and reviews companies across many sectors, from paint to cleaning products to building products.

Rainforest Alliance Certified: the Rainforest Alliance is an international non-governmental organization founded in 1987 with a specific focus to protect forests and farmers. This approach means they mostly monitor and create products that are made fairly and ethically. RA certification means a product was reviewed by third-party auditors and found to be socially, economically, and environmentally sustainable.

Shop Secondhand

As we've already covered, shopping secondhand is one of the most environmentally friendly actions you can take. And you don't need to worry about greenwashing when you get something thrifted; the raw materials have already been used, and you're likely keeping the item from a landfill.

Borrow, Trade, or Swap

Why even buy something in the first place? Lean into your community, and see if you can borrow, swap, or trade to meet your needs. Find groups on Facebook or in local community centers or religious places that organize swaps or have people open to trading.

How to Advocate for Companies to Move Beyond Greenwashing into Action

Let your voice be heard by advocating against greenwashing! When it comes to advocacy, a stat I like to keep in mind is that 70% of the US economy is consumer spending. That means that huge power lies in the hands of people like you and me. If we stop shopping, 70% of the US economy stops. Paul Dillenger, vice president of global product innovation at Levi's, told author JB MacKinnon for his book *The Day the World Stops Shopping* (2021) that people "stop shopping for a week, and it would be a market event. No shopping for a month, and this industry falls apart."

One month. One single month where no one buys new clothes and the entire fashion industry crumbles. Collective power and action makes change happen quickly.

Here is what we can do to collectively get companies beyond greenwashing and into real action.

Boycotts

A boycott is a type of protest where you withhold money, time, labor, or some sort of important item from someone or a company. This creates financial pressure on the company and brings them to the negotiation table. In 1963, Reverend Dr. Martin Luther King Jr, the Southern Christian Leadership Conference, James Bevel, and Fred Shuttlesworth led a boycott of businesses in Birmingham, Alabama, as part of their plan to desegregate the city. Birmingham was at the time commonly referred to as the most segregated city in the US.

The first wave of boycotts began in 1962, when students at Miles College arranged a year of staggered boycotts that caused downtown business to decline by as much as 40%. The second wave of boycotts in 1963 were done under Dr. King and brought national attention to the city. The boycotts focused the protests on the weeks before Easter, the second-busiest shopping season of the year for the city. Predominantly Black churchgoers, students, and citizens refrained from shopping at businesses that engaged in segregation. There were even boycott patrols, where people participating in the boycott would confront Black shoppers looking to spend money in these stores and encourage them to join the boycott. The boycott was hailed as a success, and the national attention it drew was a direct reason for the passing of the Civil Rights Act of 1964.

Boycotts fail when they get too diffuse or unclear. The best strategy is to pick one specific product or one specific company and concentrate the boycott efforts on that for a few months at a time. Reports show that boycotts with the most media attention have the largest impact, so drawing as much attention to your boycott as possible is also key. Alert traditional media, such as local news stations and newspapers, about the boycott. Post about it on social media and try to have the news amplified by getting others to share as well. The more a boycott stays in common conversation, the more people are likely to participate, especially in the long term.

Support Companies Doing Good

Just as boycotts work by withholding money from companies, financial support to companies that are not participating in greenwashing sends a message that that kind of corporate behavior is desired by consumers. A 2018 study by McKinsey found that Gen Z sees "consumption as a matter of ethical concern" (Francis and Hoefel 2018). Authenticity and honesty rank high in factors for making a purchase, and the same study found that "for Generation Z, as we have seen, the main spur to consumption is the search for truth."

Companies that share transparently about how they make their products are found to be more trustworthy and thus worthy of a dollar to younger generations. If and when you find a company that aligns with your values and doesn't participate in greenwashing, supporting them with your dollars and voice is a way to help keep that behavior going. Buy their products and share why you like them with your circles. Again, amplification works in your favor. Just as telling people why to not support a company can help a boycott, telling people why you do support a company can help an ethical brand stay in business.

Write to Companies

Sometimes companies make decisions because someone in a suit told them to, and they genuinely don't know that it's not something their audiences want. Some companies just need to be informed!

In 2015, Salesforce Personnel Chief Cindy Robbins went to the CEO with a concern: there was a wage gap at the company. CEO Marc Benioff blew her off; the company was ranked as one of the best places to work in the US, and he had personally invested in a company culture that hired and promoted women. Robbins asked for an internal audit of wages across men and women in the company, and Benioff agreed.

Turns out, there was a persistent wage gap between men and women at Salesforce. Women were chronically underpaid in every department. So Benioff kept his word, and the company spent $3 million to bring underpaid women up to equal pay with their male counterparts. More than 10% of women at the company saw an increase in their paychecks after the audit (Stahl 2018).

What Salesforce needed to make a change was the data that showed them they had a wage gap. Once they had that information, they corrected their wages accordingly. Writing, calling, or participating in social media campaigns that have direct evidence of wrongdoing is one way to get companies to change corporate practices. Supporting the voices and experiences of employees who say they've been mistreated or underpaid is a good example of this. Amplify their experiences to those in power at the company.

Put a special emphasis on writing and calling! People take other people more seriously than they do an email or a comment on an Instagram post. A direct letter or phone call, where you talk to another person, has a heavier influence on action.

Talk About It with Others

I've heard it said that there are no serial killers in the Philippines because people talk to each other too much. A serial killer requires stealth and secrecy to commit their murders. In the Philippines, people are too involved in each other's lives, spend too much time talking to one another, and know too much about each other's movements and activities for someone to get away with it.

That's what we can do to greenwashing companies. Make it too hard for them to hide by telling each other when we find a company being shady. If you know that a company has done some greenwashing, tell a friend. Post on your social media. Bring it up at dinner. Awareness is key to change, and awareness builds when people talk about things.

It can be hard to have conversations with people you love if and when you know they disagree with your stance. I like to approach those conversations with a piece of relationship advice I heard years ago: when there's a problem in your relationship, remember that it's you and your partner against the problem, not you against your partner.

Taking this mindset into conversations with people who perhaps have different political opinions than I do has been helpful. Find common ground about the problem that you can agree on. For example, I have people in my life that say they don't believe in climate change. But they do think that summers are getting hotter, and they dislike that (because who enjoys a month straight of 100° weather?). I find this to be a good point of entry to the climate change conversation, because now we're in agreement that hotter summers are bad.

CHAPTER EIGHT

ENVIRONMENTAL JUSTICE FOR ALL

There may be times when we are powerless to prevent injustice,
but there must never be a time when we fail to protest.

—Elie Wiesel

When I was a kid, my siblings and I watched a cartoon called *Captain Planet*. Captain Planet was Earth's greatest hero, who fought environmental injustice with the help of five humans from around the world. His skin was bright blue, he had a neon green mullet, and he wore a red crop-top with red elbow-length gloves. Each human hailed from a different place on the globe: Kwame from Africa, Wheeler from North America, Linka from the Soviet Union, Gir from Asia, and Ma-Ti from South America. Each human also had a ring that activated a specific power linked to an element on the Earth: water, fire, earth, air, and heart.

The five humans fought to protect the planet from environmental destruction, pollution, and confrontations between humans. When all five combined their rings, they could summon Captain Planet, who would help them give the episode's bad guy the final one–two punch. At the end of each episode, Captain Planet himself would point out at the viewers and deliver a call to environmental action. "The power is yours," he declared before returning back into the rings. My siblings and I would fight over who Captain Planet was pointing at, jockeying to be chosen as the next hero of the Earth.

In real life, we may not have a blue-skinned man with a green mullet to administer environmental justice, but we do have a long history of regular people fighting for the exact same thing.

Hazel M. Johnson began her personal fight for environmental justice in 1969, after her 41-year-old husband passed away from lung cancer. In short order, several other people from her predominantly Black community, Altgeld Gardens on the South Side of Chicago, also passed away from lung cancer. After a news story reported that Altgeld Gardens had one of the highest cancer rates in all of Chicago, Johnson found that her community was built on a former landfill and surrounded by toxic waste sites. The land and air of her home was literally poisoned. This pollution had cost her community members their lives and put Johnson herself in danger.

It was a situation for Captain Planet, but it was Johnson who spent the remainder of her life fighting to right this wrong and to bring environmental justice to not only her South Side community but also other communities of color that were dealing with environmental hazards that shortened their lifespan and came with a higher financial burden.

In 1979, Johnson founded the organization People for Community Recovery (PCR), whose mission according to their website "is to enhance the quality of life of residents living in communities affected by environmental pollution." PCR has recorded many fights and victories for communities of color in the Chicago area, including blockading entry to a landfill site where the city planned to dump toxic waste near where Black people lived on the South Side in 1987 and successfully lobbying the city to add an elderly Black community to the city's water and sewer lines in 1985, services that the citizens had been paying for without actually receiving for more than two decades.

Johnson was also instrumental in creating the 17 Principles of Environmental Justice with other environmental activists. She presented these principles to the US Congress in 1993.

1. Environmental justice affirms the sacredness of Mother Earth, ecological unity and the interdependence of all species, and the right to be free from ecological destruction.

2. Environmental justice demands that public policy be based on mutual respect and justice for all peoples, free from any form of discrimination or bias.

3. Environmental justice mandates the right to ethical, balanced and responsible uses of land and renewable resources in the interest of a sustainable planet for humans and other living things.

4. Environmental justice calls for universal protection from nuclear testing, extraction, production and disposal of toxic/hazardous wastes and poisons and nuclear testing that threaten the fundamental right to clean air, land, water, and food.

5. Environmental justice affirms the fundamental right to political, economic, cultural and environmental self-determination of all peoples.

6. Environmental justice demands the cessation of the production of all toxins, hazardous wastes, and radioactive materials, and that all past and current producers be held strictly accountable to the people for detoxification and the containment at the point of production.

7. Environmental justice demands the right to participate as equal partners at every level of decision-making including needs assessment, planning, implementation, enforcement and evaluation.

8. Environmental justice affirms the right of all workers to a safe and healthy work environment, without being forced to choose between

an unsafe livelihood and unemployment. It also affirms the right of those who work at home to be free from environmental hazards.

9. Environmental justice protects the right of victims of environmental injustice to receive full compensation and reparations for damages as well as quality health care.

10. Environmental justice considers governmental acts of environmental injustice a violation of international law, the Universal Declaration of Human Rights, and the United Nations Convention on Genocide.

11. Environmental justice must recognize a special legal and natural relationship of Native Peoples to the U.S. government through treaties, agreements, compacts, and covenants affirming sovereignty and self-determination.

12. Environmental justice affirms the need for urban and rural ecological policies to clean up and rebuild our cities and rural areas in balance with nature, honoring the cultural integrity of all our communities, and providing fair access for all to the full range of resources.

13. Environmental justice calls for the strict enforcement of principles of informed consent, and a halt to the testing of experimental reproductive and medical procedures and vaccinations on people of color.

14. Environmental justice opposes the destructive operations of multinational corporations.

15. Environmental justice opposes military occupation, repression and exploitation of lands, peoples and cultures, and other life forms.

16. Environmental justice calls for the education of present and future generations which emphasizes social and environmental issues, based on our experience and an appreciation of our diverse cultural perspectives.

17. Environmental justice requires that we, as individuals, make personal and consumer choices to consume as little of Mother Earth's

resources and to produce as little waste as possible; and make the conscious decision to challenge and reprioritize our lifestyles to insure the health of the natural world for present and future generations.

Johnson, quite literally, wrote the book on what environmental justice is. As we tackle new climate crises around the globe, we must remember that not everyone is going to experience climate crises in the same way. Not everyone will have the same resources, flexibility, or flexibility. Communities such as Altgeld Gardens are starting off in worse positions than communities like Beverly Hills, due to decades of racism, sexism, and resource hoarding.

And truly, living in a greener way as a planet and as a people means living in a more just world. We can't solve the climate crisis without acknowledging that some people have been getting the short end of the stick for generations. What's more, we can't move forward toward a greener, safer future for some while also actively leaving people behind.

I am writing this chapter in Charlotte, North Carolina. Charlotte is about a three-hour drive from Warren County, North Carolina. I'm a little biased, but North Carolina is an incredibly beautiful state, and the nature here is a point of pride for the residents. The Resource Conservation and Recovery Act (RCRA) was enacted by Congress in 1976. The RCRA gave the Environmental Protection Agency (EPA) the authority to control the generation, transportation, treatment, storage, and disposal of hazardous waste. One of the main goals for the act was to protect both human health and the natural environment from the potential hazards of waste disposal, aka keep harmful materials out of people's homes and things such as the river that runs through town.

In 1978, Ward Transformer Company, a Raleigh-based company that handled electronic gear, deliberately let 31,000 gallons of polychlorinated biphenyl (PCBs) fluid seep along 240 miles of North Carolina roadways in 14 different counties. If you're not a chemistry whiz, PCBs are sometimes referred to as "forever chemicals" because of how long-lasting they are.

They are also potentially lethal to humans and animals and have been found to cause liver disease, chronic headaches, and lower cognitive development.

After the illegal dumping was discovered, the state of North Carolina assumed responsibility for cleaning up the pollution. (Yet another instance of the taxpayer picking up the check for bad corporate behavior.) A site for the PCBs had to be chosen, and Warren County was the final decision. There were only two problems with this decision: Warren County did not have the tools or infrastructure needed to properly dispose of the PCBs, and the community was predominantly Black. Despite the passing of the RCRA, people, mostly Black people, were again being put at risk of exposure to toxic chemicals by the state legislature. The RCRA was not protecting everyone equally.

Environmental justice is something that activists such as Hazel M. Johnson have worked on loudly for decades. Many of the laws and protections already in place come from their efforts. But throughout this book, we've talked extensively about what is in our power to create change in the world. As we look toward the future, we can also take a look around and say, "Who continues the work today? Who is currently knocking it out of the park when it comes to creating a more just world? Who is out there *today* who is pursuing environmental justice?" Asking these questions and looking for answers in your own community may show you that there are already many efforts underway to create our greener world.

LAND, LIBERATION, AND A DAMN FINE TOMATO

Soul Fire Farm sits about 40 minutes northeast of Albany, New York. Over 80 acres of land, you'll find rows of native plants, flowers, and you'll notice the trees that surround the entire farm. The farm offers programs to visitors in areas such as developing carpentry skills so that you can build things such as your own raised garden beds, and community farm days, where visitors can get hands-on experiences in traditional farming techniques.

Soul Fire Farm is, in their own words, "an Afro Indigenous–centered community farm committed to uprooting racism and seeding sovereignty in the food system" (Soul Fire Farm n.d.). Environmental and social justice is woven into every seedling, every community meeting, every CSA package that is grown on the farm and given away to someone experiencing food insecurity. The team uses ancestral farming techniques and grows only native plants in a conscious effort to be as eco-friendly as possible and to bring environmental justice directly into the daily practices of the farm. Protecting the land by treating it well is central to the idea of environmental justice—through care, this land will continue to flourish and provide for the people who work it. By using ancestral farming techniques such as polyculture farming (growing two crops on the same land, which has been proven to be better for the soil and making plants less susceptible to disease) instead of mono-cropping, they help restore the land while feeding people.

For Cheryl Whilby, the co-executive director of communications and development at the farm, the concept of environmental justice goes hand in hand with building a greener world.

"I think about it this way: Who is most impacted by climate change and environmental disasters?" Cheryl tells me one February afternoon. "What do we do to make sure that our people are taken care of?"

Soul Fire Farm has done a lot in pursuit of answering that question. Soul Fire Farm Land Stewardship Collective LLC is a housing cooperative that includes all residents in decision-making using a one-member, one-vote structure. Founded in 2011 by Leah Penniman, a Black Kreyol woman, the farm team takes the approach that food is a right, a medicine, and a way to create equality in a country outright hostile to Black and Brown people. They work to help end food and land discrimination and help Black and Brown people access fresh food.

Karen Washington, a food justice advocate and farmer, coined the term "food apartheid" to draw attention to the "root causes of inequity in our food system based on race, class, and geography" (Washington n.d.). Since 1985, Washington has worked in food in the Bronx, a predominantly Black borough of New York City. While one can eat anywhere in the Bronx, the availability of fresh produce, lean meats, or non-processed food is much lower in poor areas than affluent ones. Many studies have shown that less access to fresh foods leads to a more unhealthy lifestyle, ranging from higher rates of mental illness to chronic disease to lower life expectancy. A 2005 study in Detroit found that people who live in predominantly Black and low-income neighborhoods travel an average of 1.1 miles farther to the closest supermarket than people living in predominantly White low-income neighborhoods (Two Feathers et al. 2005). This is food apartheid in action, says Washington, a food and health divide that is the result of discriminatory urban planning and policy decisions.

"It begs the question: What are the social inequities that you see, and what are you doing to address them?" asks Washington's website.

The work done at Soul Fire Farm is done to combat systems such as food apartheid. They offer farmer training for Black and Brown people living today along parts of the corridors where the Underground Railroad operated, in an effort to reconnect Black and Brown lineage to land they might have been forced off from. They also have extensive resources and guides on their website on farming, land practices, and even one guide on raising chickens in a city, for people around the world to access.

The team at the farm believes that in order to change a harmful system, you have to operate outside the system. The US is a country founded on the exploitation of Black and Indigenous labor; today Soul Fire Farm is operated by Black-led leadership and actively partners with the original inhabitants of the land, the Stockbridge Munsee Mohican Nation. There is recognition that the leadership of the farm today are themselves transplants to the land, and that true environmental justice means the involvement of the historical stewards of the land. For the last five years, the farm has worked with the members of the Stockbridge Munsee Mohican Nation (now located in Wisconsin), to allow Mohican citizens access to farmland for culture ceremonies and to harvest plants at their need.

"We lean on each other to make greatness happen," reads the farm website, and for Cheryl, these words could not be truer. Environmental justice looks like equality, and equality looks like health and freedom of movement. Together with her co-owners and colleagues at the farm, Cheryl works to restore the health of the land through farming indigenous to the area plants and focusing on feeding those most negatively affected by environmental injustice.

Cheryl and Soul Fire Farm operate on a person-to-person basis. Their efforts and aim are to transform the world immediately around them and to educate and influence anyone who comes to their farm. There are other people who are working on more systemic levels to create environmental justice for everyone.

MAKING TOP-DOWN CHANGE

Growing up in Berkeley, California, you would be hard-pressed to not become an ecologically conscious person. "My education always had an environmental component, whether it was outdoor gardening or learning about recycling, there was always something there," says Olivia Knight, racial and environmental justice manager at As You Sow. Her day-to-day job is to monitor corporate progress on racial equity, DEI disclosure, and environmental justice. A typical day in her work life is reaching out to grassroots environmental justice organizations and communities affected negatively by environmental injustice. She is the bridge between companies and communities and aims to hold a mirror up to companies that shows how their corporate decisions have real-life impacts on the people in their communities.

Being a link between companies and people has called to Olivia since she was a student at Pitzer College in Claremont, California.

"I majored in environmental analysis with a sociology focus and an Africana minor. And that really gave me the tools to come to work at a place like As You Sow because it helped me understand the global implications of environmental injustice, as well as what's happening in our own backyard. Pitzer College is in the urban sprawl empire of Los Angeles. And there are superfund sites dotted all around."

Despite their heroic-sounding names, a superfund site is the bad guy in any environmental story. Superfund sites are areas contaminated due to hazardous waste being dumped, left behind when a company closed, or otherwise improperly managed. Processing plants, landfills, and mining sites are all examples of superfund sites. They're places where companies took one thing, turned it into another, and then left or dumped the potentially toxic waste that was created in the process.

These sites can cause pollution and health problems, just as Hazel Johnson dealt with. Going to a college near so many superfund sites and studying environmental analysis lead Knight to visit these sites and the people living near them.

"And so we went to go talk with some community groups and help them get activated and energized to really face what's going on there, but also address the long-term concerns and health implications of living next to a superfund site. So personally, that's what got me started in this kind of work," shares Olivia. After college, Olivia traveled to Ghana, where her father was born and raised, where the stark differences in social classes left an impact on her. She moved to Brighton, England, to get her master's in environment, development and policy from the University of Sussex. For Olivia, the next step wasn't working with people one-on-one. She wanted to be involved with companies, working to bridge the gap between corporate action and environmental justice.

As You Sow is a nonprofit whose purpose is "to promote environmental and social corporate responsibility through shareholder advocacy, coalition building, and innovative legal strategies" (As You Sow n.d.). Their mission is twofold; As You Sow believes that corporations, under capitalism, are responsible for the biggest problems and challenges we face as a species today. In order to create a fair and sustainable world for everyone, corporations have to stop creating problems and fix the ones they've already made. To achieve that, As You Sow encourages shareholder activism, using legal means to change corporate structure, and connecting the communities harmed by corporate actions.

This is where Olivia found her professional niche. In her role, she has co-created the Racial Justice Initiative, which tracks corporate statements around promises to achieve racial equity both inside their organizations and outside, as well as DEI disclosure. The goal is to show how companies are incorporating environmental and racial justice into their corporate practices. In August 2021 As You Sow rolled out four environmental justice–focused key performance indicators (KPIs) into that racial justice scorecard.

"So really what it looked like externally was As You Sow taking on a new issue area, not only racial justice, now environmental justice. And now taking a deeper look on potential adverse effects that companies were having on BIPOC communities historically, in the past five to ten years, and then taking that to their doorstep, and telling them about our research, telling them why it matters, why it's connected to racial justice, and hopefully what they can do about it," Olivia explains.

Olivia's day-to-day work helps shed light on corporate practices for both the companies and individuals like you. She brings evidence of corporate environmental and racial malpractice to the companies themselves, to ask them to work toward correcting it. She also brings this information to the public, which allows individual investors to choose to avoid investing in these companies in their personal portfolio.

Olivia sees the impact of her work in how investors are financially reacting to companies. "I know from an investor lens, environmental justice audits, it's becoming quite an issue area with shareholder proposals. So companies are definitely getting activated and aware, which is fantastic news." In other words, money talks. The reports that Olivia helps create are driving change from individual investors, which is forcing companies to make corporate change.

THE BUY-IN: NOBODY'S FREE UNTIL EVERYBODY'S FREE

Fannie Lou Hamer declared that "Nobody's free until everybody's free" in a 1971 speech about civil rights. When we speak about environmental justice, to me it's a pretty clear goal. We can't save some parts of the world—and thus some people—and leave others behind. Nobody's free until everybody's free.

Under capitalism, what the fight for environmental justice needs the most is the social and financial buy-in from those who are doing well. As I write this, I am within walking distance of no less than four large groceries stores, at all of which I can buy a huge variety of fresh produce, organic meats, and healthy foods. I can lay safely on the grass under one of the four trees in the courtyard of my condo. I have no fear of going outside, going hungry, or being accused of not belonging in the area of my home. I'm one of the people who need to buy into helping create environmental justice for others, and you may very well be too.

It can be difficult to recognize areas of ease when you have also experienced areas of struggle. You see this a lot in the context of money with people who consider themselves self-made. Someone may have had their parents pay for college, thus receiving financial help, and then started a successful business where they worked 16-hour days for five years straight. They both had financial help and put in years of hard work. People tend to focus on the hard work and minimize the help received. They use their hard work as a shield when asked to change or even admit that they have other areas of privilege.

A phrase I find helpful when assessing my own blessings and privileges is the improv classic, "yes, and. . ." In my case, my maternal grandparents helped me pay for college, and I had to take out student loans. Yes, I lived off $10,000 a year while paying off my student loan debt, and no one has ever been racist toward me. Two things can be true at once! The "yes, and" mindset helps me see both where my life has been a challenge and the parts of my life that have never been a struggle for me. As we think about making collective change and building better systems for those most negatively affected by our current financial systems, I encourage you to apply this framework to your own life.

As with every other strategy we've talked about in this book, there are already people doing this work right now! The quilt of equality is already being sewn—it's just time for us to pick up our own needles and join in. Here's a few places to get started.

Find a Cause

Environmental justice is a topic that covers a lot of ground. Everything from building affordable housing or walkable neighborhoods to community gardens and city greenery can fall under the umbrella of environmental justice. So what do you want to work on? What fires you up, or what affects your life, family, and community? Remember for me, it was tree planting. Pick one cause and then look for people already doing that work near you.

Find a Friend

Work is better with other people! You're likely to enjoy the experience more and show up repeatedly if you're doing this with someone you like. Ask a friend, family member, coworker, or neighbor whether they want to join you next time you're volunteering or educating yourself. Remember that all work doesn't look the same; you might not be volunteering to clean trash out of a river but instead trying to educate yourself on how your city spends tax revenue. You can invite someone over to watch a live stream of the city council online with you or ask whether they want to read some articles and then discuss them with you!

Set Aside the Time

If it's on the calendar, it will get prioritized. Find a recurring time once a month to devote to this work. It doesn't have to necessarily be a huge amount of time! You can call your reps to advocate for high-speed trains in less than 15 minutes a month. The goal here is to make time to show up repeatedly for your environmental justice work and to incorporate it into the routine of your life.

Continue to Grow

Environmental justice action in your life will probably be a journey. You may spend a few years volunteering twice a month with a community garden and then experience a schedule change and no longer have that same free time. You may feel very drawn to green urban design in your 30s and then develop an interest in land restoration in your 40s. It's okay for your interests and ability to change over time! Continued growth and learning is a good thing. Let the journey take you to new places while you keep the intention for change in your heart.

CHAPTER NINE

POWER TO THE PEOPLE

The most beautiful thing about the day is that it dawns. There is always a dawn after the night has passed. Don't forget it, kids. The only losers are the ones who stop fighting.

— José Mujica Cordano

The Tongass National Forest might be where the color green was invented. Everywhere you look there are shades of green. Moss at the base of ancient trees is a deep, dark green that seems to absorb the light around it. Ferns in a bright yellow-green burst forth from the roots of fallen trees. Bold green lily pads, a shade of green I can only describe as happy, dot ponds on the edge of a tree cluster. Most of the forest's nearly 17 million acres is temperate rainforest, a type of forest that has heavy rainfall. The air is rich with the smell of soil, and a lichen in a pale, almost frosty green, called Old Man's Beard, hangs from tree branches nearly everywhere.

The forest contains some of the final remnants of the ancient glaciers that shaped North America in the last ice age. There are fjords that rise thousands of feet into the air and killer whales swim in the water. Hemlock and cedar trees that have grown to over 200 feet dot the forest.

The Tongass has been called "America's climate forest" due to the fact that it sequesters 44% of all the carbon stored by all United States' national forests (DellaSala 2021, Loki 2023, USDA Forest Service 1989). Trees store carbon by using photosynthesis to take carbon dioxide out of the air and turn it into food, which then fuels tree growth. It's a beautiful system and one that helps hugely in the fight against a warming planet. And many of the trees storing carbon for us all in this national forest are old. Scientists estimate that the old-growth trees are between 100 and 700 years old. Some of these trees were alive before the Great Depression, and some were alive before the Aztec Empire built a capital city.

Old-growth forest is the best type of forest. I don't mean to play favorites, but old-growth forest is where the magic happens. Old-growth forest has a unique structure. The diverse species of trees growing near each other offer various canopy layers for many different birds to nest in. Trees that have not been touched by human activity for hundreds of years will develop hollow cavities, which become nesting places for animals like foxes, raccoons, and porcupines. When a tree dies and falls over, its exposed roots create another home base for insects, fungi, reptiles, and amphibians. As fallen trees decay, they are one of the few places where new topsoil is created instead of destroyed. Old-growth trees store more carbon and nitrogen than younger trees. Basically, old-growth forests are entire ecosystems that run themselves very nicely and whose actions benefit people and animals around the world.

The Tongass represents something that is all too often forgotten in our fast-paced modern lives. This forest on the coast of Alaska is essential to life on the other side of the globe. While we tend to think of what matters to us, and what is important to us, as what is right in front of our faces on a daily basis, we live on a planet where we are all interconnected. The Tongass, like the Amazon or the Taiga in Russia, are like the lungs of the entire planet. They "breathe" for us all. The carbon they store helps regulate global temperatures. So if you're having a lovely 75-degree day in Rhode Island, it's in part thanks to the Tongass, some 4,150 miles away.

Unfortunately for all of us, the US-based logging industry has been consistently cutting down the old-growth forest in Tongass National Forest for the last 70 years. Between 1976 and 1996, over 50% of the old-growth forest was removed by logging ventures (USDA Forest Service 1989). The magic of the forest was being lost, with sections of the forest being totally clear-cut. To clear-cut a forest means to cut down every tree in the vicinity; if you're a '90s kid like me, imagine the scene from *Ferngully* where the fairy Crysta discovers what the humans are really doing in her home. She flies between stumps of trees that have been clear-cut and then pops up to view a whole swath of her rainforest decimated, pollution turning the air brown, and a truck of humans in yellow hard hats hauling off the now-felled trees.

In fact, humans have cut down over half of the forests on our planet in just 8,000 years (Melillo 2021). Cutting down trees releases the carbon they store and prevents them from absorbing any more in future. This adds to the warming of the planet.

From a money perspective, logging in the Tongass is a bad deal for everyone, including the logging companies. Logging costs money, and from 1980 to 2001 logging in areas of the Tongass where it's allowed cost the US government $1.96 billion, while timber sales only generated $227 million in revenue (Taxpayers for Common Sense 2020). At a loss of $40 million per year, no money nerd on earth could make the argument that it's an activity that makes sense. "It actually costs taxpayers millions to 'sell' timber that we collectively own, which makes no sense," said Autumn Hanna, vice president of Taxpayers for Common Sense, who authored the report.

In the early 1980s Indigenous groups native to the Tongass area—the Tlingit, Haida, and Tsimshian Peoples—started to protest the logging and road building that was happening in the forest. Clear-cutting was harming their way of living, which relies heavily on the lands and animals of the Tongass. For generations upon generations, Indigenous groups have eaten the beach asparagus and salmon that spawn in the forest rivers. Indigenous land practices, from cultivation to restoration, have protected and grown the forest for the 10,000 documented years that people have lived in the region.

Led by Indigenous women, the decades-long campaign began in the late 1970s and included sit-ins, marches, and letter writing to representatives. Leaders from the Tlingit, Haida, and Tsimshian dressed in traditional regalia and showed the world (and most importantly, the government) exactly how and why the Tongass served them and the state. The first major win of these efforts came in 1990, when then–President George H. W. Bush signed into law the Tongass Timber Reform Act (TTRA).

TTRA drastically increased the protection of the Tongass National Forest from the logging industry by designating roughly 856,000 acres as "roadless areas" so that large swaths of old-growth forest would remain the important ecosystems they are. The act specifically names protection for "certain lands in the Tongass National Forest in perpetuity, to modify certain long-term timber contracts, [and] to provide for [the] protection of riparian habitat" (Mrazek 1989). In what may surprise people reading this in a post-2020 world, the act was completely bipartisan and passed almost unanimously in the Senate, 99 votes to 0.

Logging was still permitted, and so the advocacy continued. Throughout the 1990s, the political debate about protecting the Tongass centered on the "roadless" areas of the park, places where no roads had been built. These are the last truly wild areas of the National Forest and Park system, since they are significantly harder to reach. Road building involves felling trees, destroying animal habitat, and killing plant life, which are all things one does not want in a forest. Builders and loggers wanted access to the area to cut the old-growth trees, and environmentalists and Indigenous groups wanted further protections to help maintain the ecological benefits these places provide.

In 2001, during the final week of his administration, President Bill Clinton passed The Roadless Rule. This law prohibits road construction or reconstruction, and timber harvesting on 58.5 million acres of cataloged "roadless" areas on National Forest System lands, including 9.2 million acres within the Tongass. The rule further protected areas of biodiversity and fragile, essential ecosystems from human interference.

The protests, the marches, the sit-ins. The in-person visits to congresspeople, the office calls, the petitions. It had worked. People who cared about protecting the Tongass had fought for the system to step up and protect the forest, and that protection had been enshrined into law. The Tongass was a protected area, the old-growth forest safe.

HOW DO YOU EAT AN ELEPHANT?

Right now, we are beholden to a system that is poisoning us and our planet. A more people-focused system wouldn't do that—or at least, not as much. I'm not asking for *perfection*, I'm just asking for *better*. The Tongass being protected is better. The Civil Rights Act is better. We can be better, and we can have a government and a social system that are *better*.

I often ask myself, "What is the point?" Not of life but of my personal efforts. What am I hoping will change by not personally investing in fossil fuels? What am I attempting to change by not eating red meat? What's the point of all this effort anyway?

I'll give myself the grace to say that my answer may change one day, but right now the point is that we *can* fucking do it. We can do whatever we want. Anything is possible. We've been doing things one way for the last 500 years, and it's not working out great. But we can change that, and

I want to see what the other option looks like. I want to live in a world where we don't have wildfire season because we stopped increasing the global temperature and we started using different land conservation techniques. I want to live in a world where we have three women presidents in a 20-year period and everyone thinks that is normal.

Throughout this whole book we've talked about how you can make your money greener and change your lifestyle. But now it's time to turn our attention to the systems that we all exist in and ask them to be better in the first place. What can we do to solve problems that hurt us all? So for our final chapter, I want to introduce you to people already doing the work to change the world around them on larger levels. These people have all taken action in their broader community or at a policy level to help create systemic changes around our climate and our economic systems.

STARTING A FREE STORE

The University of Tennessee at Knoxville (UTK) has a "free store." Nestled away in a nondescript corner of the campus, students, faculty, and staff members are welcome at the "store," where everything is free. Clothing, accessories, kitchenware, household appliances, furniture, and arts and craft supplies are some of the items that can be found at the store, which is open Monday–Friday during the school year.

Former Social Impact Coordinator Mikayla Barnett started the Free Store in 2017 after watching students dump perfectly good items into dumpsters at the end of the school year because they didn't want or need to take them home. Books, bedding, mini-fridges, were all ending up in dumpsters. Mikayla made it her mission to rescue these items, knowing that there was a need on campus of nearly 34,000 students and staff. Mikayla would take items she found in good or gently used condition, repair them if needed, and then bring them out into the middle of campus, and as people walked by, they could "shop" the stuff.

The current Social Impact Coordinator, Maggie Atchley, tells me there would "just be a big 'store' for students and really anyone to shop, like while they were going between classes, just walking to and from on their daily routine." From there, Mikayla was able to make the process slightly more formal, establishing hours and a repeat location. The idea was popular and gained enough traction that the Office of Sustainability eventually wrote a grant proposal that was approved by the University for formal funding, and they moved into a dedicated storefront space in 2022.

"We basically operate as kind of a nine-to-five thrift store, except everything's free," says Atchley.

Atchley shares that the Free Store is extremely popular with students and staff alike and that since they are donation based, the store is low-cost for the University to operate. Eleven students work in the office on work-study, helping to sort and process donations, and raise awareness of the store on campus. The store is partially funded by the University's "green fee," a $10 annual fee for in-state students ($35 for out-of-state students), which helps to power sustainability projects across campus. They continue to get grant funding as well, and of course, donations from students throughout the year. The store also works on a radical transparency basis, allowing students a voice in the operations.

"Students themselves are able to come and pitch their ideas and know exactly where the money is going. So we have monthly meetings to decide where we're going to allocate this funding, like what projects we're going to pursue for the coming months and everything, and that's open to all students, faculty and staff," says Atchley.

And the mission behind the store is growing. Atchley says, "When you're at a university level, it's a big resource, when you have 34,000 people at your university donating items daily. But otherwise, it's a simple initiative. You know, it's just taking things out and giving them back. So I feel like it should definitely proliferate. We're trying to work with a couple of nonprofits in our community to start up little satellite closets. Because sometimes we get too many donations for the amount of students that shop with us. I love to see it grow . . . there's plenty of free stores that exist without university funding."

The Free Store helps meet students' financial needs in a way that empowers them. Students come into the store and make their own decisions around which items they need, without having to reveal to any of their peers that they couldn't afford these items on their own. In 2022, the average college tuition in the US was $9,349 for in-state students and $27,023 for out-of-state students at a public four-year institution (Hanson n.d.). This is before the cost of travel to the university, the cost of furnishing a dorm room, or textbooks. College in the US is routinely criticized for being prohibitively expensive for many families; things like the Free Store make it less financially formidable. At UTK, students reported that the free nature of the store was important to them, as well as the ability to reuse items that would otherwise end up in landfill.

UTK students have been able to meet some of their living needs without money via institutional action. Through the green fee and grant funding, the sustainability office has redirected money they university already has toward the Free Store, and helped ease both the financial burden on students and the overall waste the university creates.

BIKEABLE COMMUNITIES NOW

"Part of the reason I got into planning was that I was like 'we are totally screwing up our world,' and transportation is a huge contributor to our greenhouse gas emissions," Shawna Kitzman tells me as she zooms along a highway. "And the bottom line for most municipalities or agencies is money."

Shawna has spent the last 18 years of her career working in transit. She works for a multi modal transportation planning firm that works with municipalities and government agencies. How do people move around cities and suburbs? What's the best way to get the most people across a downtown space in the most climate-friendly way? How do we balance sidewalks with businesses' needs for parking spaces? These are the kinds of questions that bounce around Shawna's head and that she tries to answer in her work with cities and municipalities.

"Multi modal, meaning really prioritizing bicycling, pedestrian, and transit-oriented transportation, as well as safety of our roadways," is how Shawna defines her work to me. Basically, fewer roads for cars and more sidewalks, bike lanes, and trains or buses to help move people around cities. This kind of work is desperately needed in the US, a hugely car-dependent nation. Japan started building a network of high-speed trains (they call their network the Shinkansen) in the mid-1960s. France introduced Train à Grande Vitesse, an intercity high-speed train system in 1981. Medellin, Colombia, considered the world's most violent city in the 1980s, opened a high-speed metro for its citizens in 1995. China, the biggest economic rival of the US, has 22,000 miles of high-speed rail. Yet the US has an almost nonexistent train infrastructure and certainly no high-speed trains that operate coast to coast.

For the last 70 years the US has focused on building roads. Highways, interstates, city roads. Roads for cars have been our infrastructure priority. And with roads come parking spaces, parking lots, and driveways, because of course we need someplace to put the car after we're done driving it. All of this requires spaces, which means cities have commonly grown outward instead of upward. As of summer 2024, Austin, Texas, is spending $4.5 billion to cover an additional 54 acres of land with highways, displacing more than 100 homes and businesses.

These kinds of numbers and plans annoy Shawna. They are short-term fixes for a long-term problem. The Environmental Protection Agency calculates that transportation is the largest contributor of US greenhouse gas emissions at 28%. More roads for more cars does nothing to solve that problem. Shawna's work, on the other hand, does. Right now Shawna is working on a project called "Ride Island" for the community of Aquidneck Island, in the state of Rhode Island. Her work is to image, design, and plan a way to connect the smallest state in the US via walkways and bikeways. In a state where 80% of all trips are less than four miles long, it's a project that just makes sense.

Shawna says that right now, there is a lot of funding for communities that have been harmed by past transit decisions, communities of color that were divided by building highways, communities that have poor air quality due to exposure to extreme car and truck exhaust; these are communities that more funding is flowing into now than ever before. And a lot of that is the result of federal decisions. The Bipartisan Infrastructure Deal, passed in 2021 by Congress, specifically earmarked money for these impacted communities. The plan is to invest $21 billion to clean up Superfund and brownfield sites, reclaim abandoned mine land, and cover abandoned oil and gas wells.

In Alabama, Louisiana, and Mississippi, $178.4 million in federal dollars will restore train service in areas that have not had passenger trains since Hurricane Katrina hit the area: $29.5 million will go to upgrading multiple bridges, rehabilitating locomotives, and improving track lines in Kentucky, and $11.5 million will go to creating the first-ever zero-exhaust-emissions locomotives at the Port of Baltimore, Maryland.

This is all money that can't be raised by a single person or nonprofit. This is work that cannot be done by simply changing lifestyle habits. It is a colossal change that requires funding on a massive level. It is the kind of money that changes a nation, creating new industries in many different places, that puts people back to work building the new or improved infrastructure that the country needs to remain connected. This kind of government spending brings with it a scale of work that no one person can ever achieve.

But the money does trickle down to people like Shawna, who will work with towns and cities to spend the money and to redesign how the cities work. Building a bridge that includes a walking path means it works for both cars and pedestrians. Creating new train stops means designing public waiting places that provide shade for the people waiting on their next train.

PROTESTS AND DIVESTMENT

For almost 50 years, the legal, social, and economic system in South Africa was something called apartheid. It was an extreme and dangerous form of segregation, where the racial minority of white people commanded the government, court systems, and media. There was a literal and legal racial hierarchy, dividing people into four racial categories: white, Indian, Colored, and Black. White South Africans owned 80% of the land in the country, and Black South Africans were forced to obtain and carry paperwork that explained their presence when in white-owned areas. The segregation was deep and overwhelming; in 1970 all Black South Africans were stripped of their South African citizenship, making it impossible for them to run for office or even live in South African cities without special permission.

It remains today one of the most egregious examples of racism and state-led discrimination in the world. And while apartheid was in power, people around the world protested it. Internally, resistance ranged from guerrilla warfare to passive strikes. Internationally, the protests began to focus on economic sanctions. Jamaica was the first country to ban goods from apartheid South Africa in 1959, with then–Jamaican chief minister Norman Manley, saying: "Since we cannot send a coloured athlete to South Africa, nor even a cricket team, with any pretense of dignity, why should we send our goods?"

In the US, student-led protests happened at campuses around the country and often had an economic focus. Perhaps the most well known is the 1985 protests at UC Berkeley, where for six weeks during the spring semester thousands of students advocated for the university to divest from their financial holdings in companies doing business with South Africa. The protests at Berkeley were inspired by photos of the violence police officers in South Africa inflicted upon protesters there.

At the time, Berkeley had $4.6 billion invested in various South African companies, more than any other US-based university. Students brought food, water, and sleeping bags to Sproul Hall and renamed the plaza "Biko Plaza" in honor of slain South African activist Steve Biko. Students protested in various ways, using sit-ins, sleep-ins, rallies. Two student groups, the UC Divestment Committee and the Campaign Against Apartheid, held daily rallies and helped to organize discussion groups among students and members of the public who came to join them. Students blocked entry to buildings and led boycotts of classes until the university agreed to divest. Police were called on the protesters, leading to 158 arrests. This rallied the larger Berkeley community, and drew more attention to the cause. Kurt Vonnegut and Alice Walker came to campus to stand with the students.

In May of 1985, almost two months after protests had first started, the university regents (the people who decide where the money goes) held a public forum to discuss divestment. Students found their actions to be unsatisfactory, and protests continued for another year. A little over a year later, in July 1986, the UC regents voted to divest $3.1 billion from companies doing business with the apartheid government. It was the largest university divestment in the country.

In 1990, Mandela was released, and he stopped over in Oakland to thank the students and faculty of Berkeley—his "blood brothers and sisters." The students had changed not just the national but the international conversation on apartheid.

Though originally met with resistance from both the university and the Berkeley City police, today these protests are a point of pride for UC Berkeley. These former students' actions are upheld as an example of the courage and the esteem of the university itself. *Here is where history is made*, is the line of thinking. *Our students change the very course of history.*

What were once thought impossible, radical, or irreverent often become the very things that we hold on high. The student protests of UC also prompted the US government to get into the divestment game. In 1986, Republican Senator William Roth (the same Senator who helped create the Roth IRA!) sponsored the Comprehensive Anti-Apartheid Act of 1986 (CAA). This law imposed sanctions against South Africa and stated five preconditions for lifting the sanctions that would essentially end the system of apartheid. The Act was originally created by Democrat Ron Dellums, a Black congressman from California.

The CAA was monumental; it was the first-ever piece of anti-apartheid legislation passed by Congress, stating, ". . . Requires U.S. policy toward South Africa to be designed to bring about the establishment of a nonracial democracy in South Africa. Declares that U.S. policy toward the victims of apartheid is to use economic, political, diplomatic, and other means to remove the apartheid system and to assist the victims of apartheid to overcome the handicaps imposed on them by apartheid" (Gray 1986).

The CAA focused specifically on economic sanctions to be imposed on South Africa until it ended apartheid. The act deliberately names trade and investment as tools to be used in pursuit of this goal, stating in "Title III: Measures by the United States to Undermine Apartheid" that goods made in or by South Africa were specifically forbidden entry to the US: "Importing from South Africa: (1) any gold coin minted in South Africa or sold by its Government; and (2) arms, ammunition, or military vehicles or any manufacturing data for such articles. Prohibits the importation of any article grown, produced, or manufactured by a South African parastatal organization (an organization owned or controlled by the South African Government other than an organization that received start-up funding from the South African Industrial Development Corporation but is now privately owned)..."

The act also eliminated the tax treaty between the US and South Africa, prohibited any US government entity from starting any new business contracts, eliminated US funding for promotion of tourism to South Africa, and banned the use of US funds "for any assistance to investment in, or any subsidy for trade with, South Africa." In short, it was a huge economic blow to South Africa from the richest country in the world. The legislation inspired similar sanctions from countries in Europe and Asia.

Nelson Mandela, one of the leaders of the apartheid resistance, was released in February 1990 after 27 years in prison. That summer, he visited Oakland, California, and specifically thanked the UC Berkeley protesters for their efforts in ending apartheid, saying, "We salute the state of California for having such a powerful, principled stand on divestment. We salute members of the International Longshoremen and Warehousemen Union Local 10, who refused to unload a South African titled ship in 1984 ...They established themselves as the front line of the anti-apartheid movement in the Bay Area as they laid the basis for the Bay Area Free South African Movement... BAFSAM also acted in concert with the University of California Faculty/Student Action for Divestment by marching onto campus in solidarity with the students.

Finally, the regents of the University of California voted to divest. We also note that throughout, BAFSAM has emphasized the demand for our freedom and that of all South African political prisoners. We celebrate with you the imminent birth of a new South Africa in which all shall be equal, irrespective of race, color, gender or creed."

YOUR TURN

You can take both direct and indirect action on changing the world. Direct meaning you can advocate to change and create regulations around production and recycling of products. Indirect meaning you can vote with your dollar and support the companies that are actually environmentally friendly.

Let's start with direct. There's almost nothing I like more than telling my elected officials they have to do better by their constituents and the planet. An elected official's job is to represent the best interest of the people who elected them. That means that you have every right to contact your representatives and tell them what is important to you! Representatives work for you, and your feedback and your vote are both ways you can let them know what you want them to do.

In the United States, the Federal Trade Commission (FTC) is in charge of monitoring false or deceiving marketing claims, which makes it the agency to contact with greenwashing complaints. Specifically, the FTC has "green guides," which are guides for companies to follow about the use of environmental marketing claims in their marketing and advertising. The green guides are to help companies avoid making environmental marketing claims that are misleading or untrue in the areas of "General Environmental Benefit, Compostable, Degradable, Ozone, Recyclable, Recycled Content, Carbon Offsets, Certifications and Seals of Approval, Free-of, Non-toxic, Made with Renewable Energy, and Made with Renewable Materials" (Federal Trade Commission 2012).

A lot of us think we have no personal power in the role of climate change, but you as an individual can report companies to the FTC if you believe they are violating the green guides, and you can also give your input to the FTC on how they should update or revise future green guides. In December 2022, the FTC put out a period of public comment of the green guides, which was an opportunity for regular Americans to say, "Hey, companies should do more of this or less of this." Feedback was open for 60 days and then closed so it could be reviewed and incorporated into updating the guides.

This is just one chance to share your voice with your government. Many groups of people have also used the legal system to create systemic change around climate action. In April 2024, a landmark legal case passed in Europe. A group of Swiss women called Senior Women for Climate

Protection sued their government for not doing enough to lower emissions, stating that it was a violation of their right to life because older women are most vulnerable to the extreme heat that is becoming more frequent in Europe and around the globe.

Europe's highest human rights court ruled in their favor, stating that countries must better protect their people from the consequences of climate change. Specifically, the court ruled that Switzerland "had failed to comply with its duties" to combat climate change and meet emissions targets, which in turn put these women's lives at risk due to the higher heat. The landmark case sets a legal precedent for future climate-based cases to be brought in any of the Council of Europe's 46 member states.

In the US, a similar case was won by young climate activists in Montana in August 2023. In *Held vs Montana*, 16 people from ages 5 to 22 alleged the state was violating their constitutional right to a clean and healthful environment by allowing and supporting fossil fuel development within the state. The activists argued that climate change–fueled events such as forest fires were a harm to their physical and mental health. Further, they argued that climate change threatened their future, with rising drought making growing food harder and drying out rivers that provided for wildlife and agriculture. In August 2023, a Montana judge ruled in their favor, finding that the state's ongoing enthusiastic investments into fossil fuels were violating their constitutional right to a clean and healthful environment, now and in the future.

As a single person you can vote and lobby for legislation that takes climate change seriously. Groups such as Citizens Climate Lobby (CCL) help organize people to advocate for legislative change around climate problems such as emissions. In spring of 2024, the group focused on mobilizing people to call and write to their representatives supporting the Energy Innovation and Carbon Dividend Act (H.R.5744). The Act charges corporate fossil fuel companies a fee for the carbon pollution they put into the air and then gives that money to Americans in the form of monthly payments. In June, CCL has an annual conference in Washington, DC, where it gathers members from around the country to actually go in person to visit representatives and advocate in person, together, for climate legislation. CCL has 530 local chapters in the US and is global, so you don't have to do this work alone.

You can use your voice. Whether you write, call, run for office, or protest to someone already in office, there are myriad ways to communicate the vision you have for the world, and how your money gets spent by those in charge.

EPILOGUE

In 1930, John Maynard Keynes penned an essay titled "Economic Possibilities for Our Grandchildren." In it, Keynes, who would become one of the most influential economists of the 20th century, predicted that in 100 years, people would only work 15 hours per week. Keynes made such a bold prediction by looking at the data in front of him. Technology was advancing, and surely that, combined with machine work, would lead to humans needing to put in fewer hours at work.

Keynes predicted what we might call a return to "the simple life," one where people have all they need to live, work to maintain that, and that is enough. A 15-hour workweek would be the necessary amount to satisfy both people's financial and personal needs. Nothing more would be needed, and free time would become the main occupation for humans. And he expected this change to come about within two generations.

Two generations. Such a short time frame for massive change. What could we, today, change in two generations? What will the world be like for my grandchildren? Will we leave them a landscape ravaged by climate change? Or will they continue the legacy of change that started here, with us?

We need to change what we're doing, and where we put our money is the most important first step. And while that seems daunting at first, it's also exactly what we as a species have been doing since the dawn of humankind. Before we had cars, we had horse-drawn carriages. When the car was invented, we made adjustments in our world: we paved roads, added driveways to homes, and installed stoplights. Humans lived without indoor plumbing for most of history. When we figured it out, we added the pipes and sewer systems to our cities that it required. Change *is* the human experience.

I've thought a lot about how I might end this book, and the best I think I have for you is this: your dollar is powerful, and I hope you keep that in mind when you spend it. Every dollar you spend, save, or invest is a vote to shape the world. Whatever it is you want to see, do, or be in this world, you can do it, and there are probably people already living that way out there. Find them, join them, and make changes together. Nothing needs to be done alone, in the darkness. Together we can reimagine our world, and together, our money can bring that re-creation to life.

REFERENCES

As You Sow. n.d. "As You Sow: Nation's Non-Profit Leader in Shareholder Advocacy." Accessed June 16, 2024. https://www.asyousow.org/about-us.

BankingOnClimateChaos.org. 2024. "Banking on Climate Chaos: Fossil Fuel Finance Report 2024." https://www.bankingonclimatechaos.org/?bank=JPMorgan%20Chase#fulldata-panel.

Baten, J. 2016. *A History of the Global Economy 1500 to Present*. Cambridge University Press.

Bell, J., Poushter, J., Fagan, M., and Huang, C. 2021. "Climate Change Concerns Make Many Around the World Willing to Alter How They Live and Work." Pew Research Center. September 14, 2021. https://www.pewresearch.org/global/2021/09/14/in-response-to-climate-change-citizens-in-advanced-economies-are-willing-to-alter-how-they-live-and-work/.

Brady, D., Kohler, U., and Zheng, H. 2023. "Novel Estimates of Mortality Associated With Poverty in the US." *JAMA Internal Medicine* 183 (6): 618–619. https://doi.org/10.1001/jamainternmed.2023.0276.

Care.com Editorial Staff. 2024. "This Is How Much Child Care Costs in 2024." Care.Com Resources (blog). January 17, 2024. https://www.care.com/c/how-much-does-child-care-cost/.

ClientEarth. n.d. "About Us | ClientEarth." Accessed June 16, 2024. https://www.clientearth.us/about-us/.

Cox, J. 2020. "Retail Sales Plunge a Record 16.4% in April, Far Worse than Predicted." CNBC. May 15, 2020. https://www.cnbc.com/2020/05/15/us-retail-sales-april-2020.html.

Davis, L., and Parker, K. 2019. "A Half-Century after 'Mister Rogers' Debut, 5 Facts about Neighbors in the U.S." Pew Research Center (blog). August 15, 2019. https://www.pewresearch.org/short-reads/2019/08/15/facts-about-neighbors-in-u-s/.

DellaSala, Dominick. 2021. "Protecting the Tongass Rainforest, Older Forests, and Large Trees Nationwide for the U.S. Nationally Determined Contribution to the Paris Climate Agreement." Wild Heritage: A Project of Earth Island Institute. https://wild-heritage.org/wp-content/uploads/2021/03/DellaSala-2021-Tongass.pdf.

Deloitte Global. 2023. "Mental Health Today—A Deep Dive Based on the 2023 Gen Z and Millennial Survey."

DePillis, L. 2019. "Fast, Free Shipping Has an Environmental Cost | CNN Business." July 15, 2019. https://www.cnn.com/2019/07/15/business/fast-shipping-environmental-impact/index.html.

EPA. 2016. "Frequent Questions: EPA's Greenhouse Gas Equivalencies Calculator." Overviews and Factsheets. December 12, 2016. https://www.epa.gov/energy/frequent-questions-epas-greenhouse-gas-equivalencies-calculator.

Federal Trade Commission. 2012. "Guides for the Use of Environmental Marketing Claims; Final Rule." Federal Register.

Francis, T., and Hoefel, F. 2018. "Generation Z Characteristics and Its Implications for Companies | McKinsey." November 12, 2018. https://www.mckinsey.com/industries/consumer-packaged-goods/our-insights/true-gen-generation-z-and-its-implications-for-companies.

Gray, Rep. W. H., III [D-PA-2]. 1986. *Summary: H.R.4868—Comprehensive Anti-Apartheid Act of 1986.*

Griffin, P. 2017. "CDP Carbon Majors Report 2017." CDP, Climate Accountability Institute. https://cdn.cdp.net/cdp-production/comfy/cms/files/files/000/000/979/original/Carbon-Majors-Database-2017-Method.pdf.

Guzman, G., and Kollar, M. 2023. "Income in the United States: 2022." Census. Gov. September 12, 2023. https://www.census.gov/library/publications/2023/demo/p60-279.html.

Hanson, M. n.d. "Average Cost of College by State [2023]: Tuition + Fees." Education Data Initiative. Accessed June 16, 2024. https://educationdata.org/average-cost-of-college-by-state.

Haqqi, S. 2022. "The Most Popular Fashion Brands around the World | Money.Co.Uk." November 30, 2022. https://www.money.co.uk/credit-cards/most-popular-fashion-brands-2022.

Hernandez Kent, A., and Ricketts, L. 2024. "The State of U.S. Wealth Inequality." May 3, 2024. https://www.stlouisfed.org/institute-for-economic-equity/the-state-of-us-wealth-inequality.

Hickel, J. 2020. *Less Is More: How Degrowth Will Save the World*. London: Penguin Random House.

Hickman, Elizabeth Marks, Susan Clayton, Panu Pihkala, R. Eric Lewandowski, Elouise Mayall, Britt Wray, Catriona Mellor, and Lise van Susteren. 2021. "Climate Anxiety in Children and Young People and Their Beliefs about Government Responses to Climate Change: A Global Survey." University of Helsinki, Helsinki Institute of Sustainability Science (HELSUS).

Inman, J. J., and Winer, R. S. 1998. *Where the Rubber Meets the Road: A Model of In-Store Consumer Decision Making*. Marketing Science Institute.

Laville, S. 2019. "Coca-Cola Admits It Produces 3m Tonnes of Plastic Packaging a Year." *The Guardian*, March 14, 2019. https://www.theguardian.com/business/2019/mar/14/coca-cola-admits-it-produces-3m-tonnes-of-plastic-packaging-a-year.

Lindsay, R. 2024. "Climate Change: Atmospheric Carbon Dioxide | NOAA Climate. Gov." April 9, 2024. http://www.climate.gov/news-features/understanding-climate/climate-change-atmospheric-carbon-dioxide.

Loki, R. 2023. "The Case for Protecting the Tongass National Forest, America's 'Last Climate Sanctuary.'" Socialist Project: The Bullet. November 5, 2023. https://socialistproject.ca/2023/11/case-for-protecting-the-tongass-national-forest/.

MacKinnon, J. B. 2021. *The Day the World Stops Shopping: How Ending Consumerism Saves the Environment and Ourselves*. HarperCollins.

Markides, C. C., and Berg, N. 1988. "Manufacturing Offshore Is Bad Business." *Harvard Business Review*, September 1, 1988. https://hbr.org/1988/09/manufacturing-offshore-is-bad-business.

Mattila, A., and Wirtz. J. 2008. "The Role of Store Environmental Stimulation and Social Factors on Impulse Purchasing." *Journal of Services Marketing* 22.

Melillo, J. 2021. "Forests and Climate Change." MIT Climate Portal. October 7, 2021. https://climate.mit.edu/explainers/forests-and-climate-change.

Mrazek, Rep. Robert J. [D-NY-3]. 1989. *H.R.987—Tongass Timber Reform Act*.

Murray, S. H. 2022. "How Affluence Pulls People Away from Their Families." *The Atlantic*. May 11, 2022. https://www.theatlantic.com/family/archive/2022/05/living-close-to-family-parents/629819/.

Murthy, V. H. 2023. "Our Epidemic of Loneliness and Isolation 2023."

National Homelessness Law Center. 2021. "Housing Not Hadcuffs 2012: State Law Supplement."

National Institute on Aging. 2020. "Goal B: Better Understand the Effects of Personal, Interpersonal, and Societal Factors on Aging, Including the Mechanisms through Which These Factors Exert Their Effects." NIH, National Institute on Aging. https://www.nia.nih.gov/about/aging-strategic-directions-research/goal-behavioral-psychological-factors.

Nixon, R. 1973. "Address to the Nation About Policies to Deal with the Energy Shortages." The American Presidency Project. https://www.presidency.ucsb.edu/documents/address-the-nation-about-policies-deal-with-the-energy-shortages.

Rodriguez, M., and Leinberger, C. 2023. "Foot Traffic AHEAD: Ranking Walkable Urbanism in America's Largest Metros 2023." Smart Growth America Places Platform, LLC.

Soul Fire Farm. n.d. "Mission." Accessed June 16, 2024. https://www.soulfirefarm.org/.

St. Louis Federal Reserve. 2024. "Survey of Household Economics and Decisionmaking in 2023." Consumer and Community Research Section of the Federal Reserve Board's Division of Consumer and Community Affairs. 2024.

Stahl, L. 2018. "Salesforce CEO Marc Benioff: Leading by Example to Close the Gender Pay Gap." *CBS News*, April 15, 2018. https://www.cbsnews.com/news/salesforce-ceo-marc-benioff-leading-by-example-to-close-the-gender-pay-gap/.

Synthetics Anonymous 2.0. 2023. "Synthetics Anonymous: Fashion's Persistent Plastic Problem." Changing Markets.

Taxpayers for Common Sense. 2020. "New Report: Taxpayers Lost $1.7 Billion from Money-Losing Timber Sales in the Tongass over Last Four Decades." September 2, 2020. https://www.taxpayer.net/energy-natural-resources/new-report-taxpayers-losing-hundreds-of-millions-of-dollars-on-tongass-timber-sales-over-last-two-decades-2/.

Thanhauser, S. 2022. "A Brief History of Mass-Manufactured Clothing." *Literary Hub* (blog). January 27, 2022. https://lithub.com/a-brief-history-of-mass-manufactured-clothing/.

Toyota Blog. 2021. "15 Years of the Toyota Prius: Toyota UK Magazine." Accessed June 16, 2024. https://mag.toyota.co.uk/15-years-of-the-toyota-prius/.

Trees Charlotte. 2022. "TreesCharlotte | 2022 Tree Canopy Assessment." https://treescharlotte.org/tree-education-resources/charlotte-tree-resources/.

Two Feathers, J., Kieffer, E. C., Palmisano, G., Anderson, M., Sinco, B., Janz, N., Heisler, M., Spencer, M., Guzman, R., Thompson, J. and Wisdom, K. 2005. "Racial and Ethnic Approaches to Community Health (REACH) Detroit Partnership: Improving Diabetes-Related Outcomes Among African American and Latino Adults." *American Journal of Public Health*, September.

Tyson, A., Funk, C., and Kennedy, B. 2023. "What the Data Says about Americans' Views of Climate Change." *Pew Research Center* (blog). August 9, 2023. https://www.pewresearch.org/short-reads/2023/08/09/what-the-data-says-about-americans-views-of-climate-change/.

U.S. Fish and Wildlife Service. 2023. "21 Species Delisted from the Endangered Species Act Due to Extinction | U.S. Fish & Wildlife Service." October 16, 2023. https://www.fws.gov/press-release/2023-10/21-species-delisted-endangered-species-act-due-extinction.

UN Environment Programme. n.d. "Plastics Pollution Toolkit—About." UNEP Law and Environment Assistance Platform. Accessed June 16, 2024. https://leap.unep.org/en/content/basic-page/plastics-pollution-toolkit-about.

UN Environment Programme. 2024. "Plastic Pollution." https://www.unep.org/plastic-pollution.

UN. 2023. "It's Official: July 2023 Was the Warmest Month Ever Recorded." UN News. 2023. August 8, 2023. https://news.un.org/en/story/2023/08/1139527.

UNCTAD. 2022. "Global Plastics Trade Hits Record $1.2 Trillion." November 10, 2022. https://unctad.org/data-visualization/global-plastics-trade-reached-nearly-1.2-trillion-2021.

US Census Bureau. 2022. "CHARS: Current Data." 2022. https://www.census.gov/construction/chars/current.html.

US Census Bureau. 2023. "U.S. Census Bureau QuickFacts: Wellesley CDP, Massachusetts." July 1, 2023. https://www.census.gov/quickfacts/fact/table/wellesleycdpmassachusetts/PST045223.

US Census Bureau. 2024. "National Poverty in America Awareness Month: January 2024." Census.Gov. January 2024. https://www.census.gov/newsroom/stories/poverty-awareness-month.html.

US Department of Defense. 2024. "Department of Defense Releases the President's Fiscal Year 2025 Defense Budget." March 11, 2024. https://www.defense.gov/News/Releases/Release/Article/3703410/department-of-defense-releases-the-presidents-fiscal-year-2025-defense-budget/.

US Energy Information Administration. 2023. "Petroleum Supply Annual, Volume 1."

USDA Forest Service. 1989. "Environmental Impact Statement USDA Forest Service 1989."

Washington, K. n.d. "FAQ." Accessed June 16, 2024. https://www.karenthefarmer.com/faq-index.

Wellesley Housing Development Corporation. 2022. "Wellesley Market Study 2022."

World Bank. 2019. "How Much Do Our Wardrobes Cost to the Environment?" World Bank. September 23, 2019. https://www.worldbank.org/en/news/feature/2019/09/23/costo-moda-medio-ambiente.

ACKNOWLEDGMENTS

In the big–picture view of life, this book and I owe a debt to every author who shaped my childhood and taught me that books can help you fly. I learned to love reading at a young age thanks to the works of people such as Tamora Pierce, Lucy Maud Montgomery, Jean Craighead George, and Scott O'Dell. Thank you for teaching me the wonder of the natural world and the power of the written word.

I'd like to deeply thank everyone I was fortunate enough to interview for this book. Your contributions helped shape this book into what it is, and the way you navigate your lives is inspiring. I hope I have done you each justice.

To my wonderful agent, Jess d'Arbonne, thanks for calling me out of the blue and saying you believed me to be an author, and thanks for rolling with me when I completely threw out our first proposal and created a new one. You are a rock star, and I am eternally grateful to you.

To Tbone, what can I say here that I don't tell you daily already? I love you, and thank you for your support and encouragement, even through my editing breakdown. You're my favorite person.

The editing team: Lori, Aldo, Premkumar, Vithusha, and my editor at Wiley, Judith. Thank you all for your help and support in creating this book.

I wouldn't be who I am without the influence and support of my grandparents, Daniel and Eileen and Dante and Altagracia. You all gave me shoulders to stand on so that I could see new heights.

Mrs. Bowe, you knew it would happen one day, and here we are. Book number one, in the bag!

And finally, to the reader. To everyone who bought a copy of this book. Thank you. Please know I wrote this from a fervent need to talk about these things, not just at the dinner table and in the car, but with people who also care, and who also feel stressed, and who also want to find like minded folks. I am so thankful to be in community with you and so glad you spent your time in these pages with me.

ABOUT
THE AUTHOR

Kara Pérez is an award-winning financial educator, first-gen Latina, and sustainability nerd. After living at the poverty line in Austin, Texas, and working five part-time jobs to pay off her student loan debt, she dove head-first into the money world to make it more accessible, sustainable, and understandable for everyone.

Kara teaches personal finance with a focus on sustainable living and climate awareness for employee resource groups, university students, and nonprofit organizations and on her website, *bravelygo.co.*

In her free time, you can find her planting trees, rewatching comfort shows, and hosting book swaps. She lives in Massachusetts with her partner, Tbone.

You can find Kara online under the handles @webravelygo on Instagram, Tiktok, and YouTube.

INDEX